"Two trustworthy theologians team up on a project to explain why it's never enough to say that the persons of the Trinity team up on projects. There is a much deeper unity to the work of the triune God, and this short, readable book directs our attention to it."

Fred Sanders, Professor of Theology, Torrey Honors College, Biola University; author, *The Deep Things of God*

"The doctrine of the inseparable operations of the Trinity is part of the deposit of the church's ancient faith. Sadly, much of contemporary evangelical thought and preaching is drifting away from this historic doctrine, unflinchingly affirmed by the theologians of the Reformation, and substituting the church's Trinitarian monotheism with a functional tritheism. The recent evangelical retrieval of this doctrine, while salutary, has not yet trickled down to the ordinary understanding of the faith. Emerson and Smith are proposing to meet that need and present inseparable operations in a way that is accessible and clearly biblical. One could not wish for a better team of Trinitarian theologians to undertake such an essential task."

Adonis Vidu, Andrew Mutch Distinguished Professor of Theology, Gordon-Conwell Theological Seminary; author, *The Same God Who Works All Things*

"Emerson and Smith describe the unity and distinction inherent in the Trinity as it unfolds across the canon of Scripture and as it develops historically by drawing from the work of the church fathers and resulting creeds. Emerson and Smith's framework reinforces the importance of a Trinitarian hermeneutic for understanding the missional authority of the triune God. This is an important book, and I am grateful for their contribution."

Cas Monaco, Vice President of Missiology and Gospel Engagement, FamilyLife

"Emerson and Smith have written a timely and helpful book for teachers, students, and church members. Though they address technical issues—Trinity, inseparable operations, appropriations, processions and missions, prosopological exegesis—they do so in an accessible manner. This book makes clear the importance of maintaining the doctrine of inseparable operations in order to maintain the biblical and historically orthodox confession of the Trinity."

Richard C. Barcellos, Pastor, Grace Reformed Baptist Church, Palmdale, California; Associate Professor of Exegetical Theology, International Reformed Baptist Seminary; author, *Trinity and Creation: A Scriptural and Confessional Account*

"Emerson and Smith provide a powerful reminder of why it is vital that we think in terms of the triune God—Father, Son, and Holy Spirit—acting in history. This book offers fresh eyes to see how all three persons of the Trinity act as one and offers hope for everything that our triune God wants to do in us and in the world."

Beth Stovell, Professor of Old Testament and Chair of General Theological Studies, Ambrose Seminary

Beholding the Triune God

The Inseparable Work of Father, Son, and Spirit

Matthew Y. Emerson and
Brandon D. Smith

WHEATON, ILLINOIS

Beholding the Triune God: The Inseparable Work of Father, Son, and Spirit

© 2024 by Matthew Y. Emerson and Brandon D. Smith

Published by Crossway
   1300 Crescent Street
   Wheaton, Illinois 60187

Cover design: Faceout Studio, Spencer Fuller

First printing 2024

Printed in the United States of America

Trade paperback ISBN: 978-1-4335-7794-9
ePub ISBN: 978-1-4335-7797-0
PDF ISBN: 978-1-4335-7795-6

Library of Congress Cataloging-in-Publication Data

Names: Emerson, Matthew Y., 1984– author. | Smith, Brandon D., author.

Title: Beholding the triune God : the inseparable work of Father, Son, and Spirit / Matthew Y. Emerson and Brandon D. Smith.

Description: Wheaton, Illinois : Crossway, [2024] | Includes bibliographical references and index.

Identifiers: LCCN 2023040568 (print) | LCCN 2023040569 (ebook) | ISBN 9781433577949 (trade paperback) | ISBN 9781433577956 (pdf) | ISBN 9781433577970 (epub)

Subjects: LCSH: Trinity. | God—Fatherhood. | Son of God. | Holy Spirit.

Classification: LCC BT111.3 .E438 2024 (print) | LCC BT111.3 (ebook) | DDC 231/.044—dc23/eng/20240220

LC record available at https://lccn.loc.gov/2023040568

LC ebook record available at https://lccn.loc.gov/2023040569

---

*To our wives, Alicia and Christa, who daily
help us behold the triune God*

Contents

Introduction

Indivisible and Undivided

IMAGINE THAT YOU'RE TRYING to describe what God did on the cross. What do you say? Here's how we've heard it described (including, at times, by ourselves!):

- The Father poured out his wrath on the Son.
- The Father turned his face away.
- The Father abandoned his Son.
- The Son felt the pangs of hell because he was separated from the Father on the cross.

Notice that in describing the cross this way, we are saying that there are two primary actors, two distinct individuals, the Father and the Son, the first two persons of the Godhead, and that each is doing something different at the crucifixion. For now, notice also that the third person of God, the Spirit, is never mentioned in these statements.

Let's use a different example. You're asked to describe God's providence. What do you say? Here's how we've heard it described (again, at times, by ourselves!):

- The Father chose this path for me because he cares for me.
- When we talk about election, we're talking about the plan of God the Father.
- We have a good Father who has planned all things to work together for our good.

Notice that in describing providence this way, we're attributing God's "plan" specifically to God the Father, and sometimes it sounds as if it's *only* God the Father who plans out providence.

One last example will suffice. Imagine that you're told to describe how a Christian receives and uses spiritual gifts. What do you say?

- The Spirit gave me the gift of [X, Y, or Z].
- I can [use gift X, Y, or Z] because the Spirit empowers me.
- I'm gifted at [X, Y, or Z] because the Spirit chose to make me that way.

Are the Father and the Son involved in the spiritual gifts? Or just the Spirit?

In each of these examples, and even in the way we've asked the follow-up questions, what we're trying to help you see is that we often think about God's acts as *divisible between the persons* and *distributed according to their roles*. So in these scenarios, sometimes the actor is primarily the Father, as in the examples about providence; sometimes the actor is the Son, as in the examples about the crucifixion; and sometimes the actor is the Spirit, as in the examples about the spiritual gifts.

Let's return to the examples related to the crucifixion. A question we often ask our students when talking about this subject, and after we've described the crucifixion in the ways we gave above, is, "What was the Spirit doing while the Father was forsaking the Son?" Was the Spirit just watching from the sidelines? Was he taking a break from his divine duties? Are the Son and the Spirit also wrathful toward sin? Returning next to providence, do the Son and the Spirit sit on the bench while the Father governs his creation? And with respect to the spiritual gifts, do the Father and the Son renounce their authority and hand it over to the Spirit to let him distribute gifts to whom he wills?

These questions, we hope, help us see that the way we talk about God's acts often divides the persons of God in a way that is contrary to our confession that God is one God in three persons. If only one divine person, or in some cases two of the three, is acting on any given occasion, how is that consistent with the Christian confession of one God, or with its roots in Jewish monotheism? Aren't there now three Gods, each of whom acts in different ways in different times? Or is there one God who is sometimes Father, sometimes Son, and sometimes Spirit? The former example is the heresy called "tritheism," while the latter is called "modalism." These are ancient false teachings that the church combatted through articulating what we know as the doctrine of the Trinity. And in order to combat them, we need to recover what the early church referred to as the doctrine of *inseparable operations*.[1] As we will see, the triune God's work in the world enables us to behold his power and goodness.

Beholding the Triune God through His Inseparable Operations

The triune God has graciously revealed himself to us. Historically and on biblical grounds, Christians have held two affirmations about who and what God is—God is one God, and he exists as three persons. This identification of God as triune stands at the heart of the Christian faith, along with the confession that the second person of the Trinity, the Son, took on a human nature without ceasing to be God. As fully human and fully God, Jesus Christ lived a perfectly righteous human life, died a penal, sacrificial, atoning death for sinners on the cross, proclaimed victory over death during his descent to the dead, and rose from the dead bodily on the third day. All of this was according to the Scriptures (1 Cor. 15:1–4) and in order to fulfill the promise that God made to Adam and Eve, that through the seed of woman he would crush the enemy's head and thereby reconcile himself to his image bearers and restore creation (Gen. 3:15).

But we would be mistaken if we took the Son's incarnation and subsequent saving actions as evidence that only *he* is acting in the

---

1 Athanasius of Alexandria offers one of the earliest accounts of a full-blown doctrine of inseparable operations. See *Epistles to Serapion* 1.1.2–3 and Lewis Ayres's discussion in *Nicaea and Its Legacy: An Approach to Fourth-Century Trinitarian Theology* (Oxford, UK: Oxford University Press, 2004), 214. In terms of modern works expounding a helpful biblical, theological, and historical doctrine of inseparable operations, nothing currently on offer compares to Adonis Vidu, *The Same God Who Works All Things: Inseparable Operations in Trinitarian Theology* (Grand Rapids, MI: Eerdmans, 2021).

act of redemption. On the contrary, it is the *one God*—Father, Son, and Spirit—who acts in the whole history of salvation, including in the incarnation. Likewise, we should remember that it is this same *one God*—Father, Son, and Spirit—who "in the beginning created the heavens and the earth" (Gen. 1:1), who called Abram out of Ur of the Chaldeans, who spoke to Moses in the burning bush, who brought Israel out of Egypt, who revealed himself to Moses and gave the Torah on Mount Sinai, who led Israel through the wilderness, who scattered Israel's enemies before her as she entered the promised land, who raised up judges and kings for Israel, who judged Israel and sent her into exile through the same nations that deserve and will receive his judgment, and who, to return to where we started, brought salvation to Israel and the nations in the person of the incarnate Son, Jesus Christ. It is this same *one God*—Father, Son, and Spirit—who calls his church together and feeds them with word and sacrament, who governs the world and brings rain on the just and the unjust, and who will, on the last day, remake what he has made and dwell with his people forever in the new heavens and new earth. In sum, the fundamental confession of God's people—"Hear, O Israel: The LORD our God, the LORD is *one*" (Deut. 6:4)— is still true even after the sending of the Son and the Spirit.

In articulating the acts of God this way, we are again emphasizing the *unity* of their action. We want to hammer this concept home at the beginning because it is one of the two major emphases of this book, and also because so much of our talk about God in contemporary evangelicalism actually cuts against God's unity, especially as it pertains to what he does. Our songs and hymns and spiritual songs, our devotional readings, our prayers, and our sermons often isolate one of the persons of God from among the other two and speak of that one person as if he is the only one carrying out a particular act (or possessing a particular attribute). The problem with this approach, where God's acts can be divvied up among the persons, is that it defies the logic of the Bible, Christian history, and systematic theology. The Bible speaks again and again of *God* acting. Systematic theology insists that for God to truly be *one*, his acts must be one, carried out by the one God who is Father, Son, and Spirit. And Christian history has taught throughout the last two millennia that the external works of God are indivisible.

Put simply: the doctrine of *inseparable operations* teaches that you cannot separate the acts of God between the persons of God. Every act of God is a singular act of Father, Son, and Spirit. So we can't say that the Father alone creates or governs or pours out his sole wrath on Jesus at the cross. We can't say that the Son alone saves us from our sins. We can't say that the Spirit alone guides or comforts or gifts believers. Why? Because they are all acts of God. Thus, every act of God is the act of the one God—Father, Son, and Spirit, singular not only in purpose or agreement, but also in essence and every divine attribute. As Gregory of Nyssa explained:

Whatever your thought suggests to you as the Father's mode of being . . . you will think also of the Son, and likewise of the Spirit. For the principle of the uncreated and of the incomprehensible is one and the same, whether in regard to the Father or the Son or the Spirit. For one is not more incomprehensible and uncreated and another less so.[2]

2 *Letter 38* 3e–3f. English translation from *Nicene and Post-Nicene Fathers*, 2nd Series, vol. 8, ed. Philip Schaff and Henry Wace, trans. Blomfield Jackson (Buffalo, NY: Christian Literature, 1895).

Put simply, Father, Son, and Spirit are each God but are not each other. To speak of any person is to speak of God, and to speak of God is to speak of three persons. It is one of the two main burdens of this book to demonstrate this claim from Scripture, theological reason, and Christian tradition.

Preserving the Properties of Each Person

The other burden of this book is to show that every act of God is the work of the *triune God*—Father, Son, and Spirit. That is, even while we emphasize the unity of God's being and therefore of God's acts, we also must insist that God is one precisely in the fact that he is three persons, and therefore that he acts as the one God who exists in three persons. In other words, it is Father, Son, and Spirit who act in every act of God, even if none of them act in isolation from each other. How can this be the case? How can we affirm that God's acts are *one*, via the doctrine of inseparable operations, but also affirm that his acts are carried out by the *three* persons? Further, how does the doctrine of inseparable operations square with the kind of language that we see in Scripture, such as the Spirit distributing spiritual gifts, or the incarnate Son saying, "Not as I will, but as you will" (Matt. 26:39)?

Regarding the former example, the church historically has relied on the doctrine of *appropriations*. That is, it is biblically sound and theologically faithful to appropriate, or attribute, particular acts of God to one of the persons of God. When we do so, we are not saying that it is only that one person who carries out that act, but we are saying that the act is uniquely associated with the mission of that one person. So, for instance, yes, it is only the Son who becomes incarnate. In this sense, the act of redemption, specifically through the incarnate Son's penal substitutionary death, is appropriated to the Son. Jesus saves! But it would be a mistake to say that because only the Son becomes incarnate, *only* the Son saves. Instead, we should say that the one act of salvation is carried out by the one God—Father, Son, and Spirit—in a way that reveals the unique personal properties of each. The Father sends the Son, the Son is sent by the Father, and the Spirit is the agent through whom the Father sends the Son. It is the Father who sends the Son to the virgin's womb, the Son who takes on human flesh in the virgin's womb, and the Spirit who causes the virgin to miraculously conceive the incarnate Son.

Order in the Trinity

Another more technical way to say this is that the divine missions are appropriated to each person according to their divine procession. To understand what this sentence means, we need to break down the vocabulary a bit.

- *Divine Simplicity.* This phrase asserts the absolute unity of the Trinity. Father, Son, and Spirit are not "parts" of God as though they each make up one-third of God's nature or essence, for the triune God is not a created being that was put together by a greater creator, but rather is eternally the one God in three persons. All of God's attributes are shared equally and fully by each person of the Trinity, which means that Father, Son, and Spirit equally *are* loving, just, powerful, authoritative, and so on. They do not sit around a divine boardroom table and discuss their "plans" or divvy up their divinity, but are rather always united in will, purpose, action, and essence.

- *Divine Processions.* This phrase refers to how God is one God in three persons from eternity. God is not divided into three persons through differences in actions or attributes or deserved adoration, but only through what are called the "eternal relations of origin." These relations refer to how each person of God subsists in the divine essence, which they equally share and together are. The Father is eternally unbegotten; that is, he does not receive the divine essence from one of the other persons. The Son is eternally begotten of the Father; that is, the Son eternally (without beginning or end) receives the divine essence from the Father; and the Spirit is eternally spirated ("breathed"); that is, the Spirit eternally receives the divine essence from the Father and the Son. Again, this generation and spiration is *eternal*, so whatever it means for the Son to be "begotten" and the Spirit to be "breathed," it's not an event that happened in time, and the persons are therefore not created.

- *Eternal Relations of Origin and* Taxis. Father, Son, and Holy Spirit are distinguished from one another eternally via relations to one another. Further, there is a *taxis* ("order") to the eternal relations of origin. The eternal relations of origin, wherein the Father is, we could say, the fount of divinity who begets the Son and who with the Son spirates the Spirit, pattern the order of God's acts. Every act of God, because of who God is as Father, Son, and Spirit, is from the Father, through the Son, and by the Spirit. And this from-through-by language does not indicate a hierarchy, but rather a unified order.

- *Divine Missions.* This phrase refers to the external works of God and their attribution to particular divine persons in the economy of salvation. The divine missions are revelations and extensions of the divine processions, the manifestation of divine persons in creation. This term, then, relates particularly to the Son, who is begotten by the Father in all eternity, being sent by the Father in the incarnation, and to the Holy Spirit, who eternally proceeds from the Father and the Son, being sent by the Father and the Son at Pentecost.

- *Appropriation.* This term refers to our ability to assign one act or attribute of God to a particular divine person while recognizing that the act or attribute to which we're referring actually belongs equally to all three at once because they are the one God.

We hope that these terms will become clearer as they are put to use in the following chapters. However, the doctrine of creation can serve as an example to start.

The Bible begins with these words: "In the beginning, *God* created the heavens and the earth" (Gen. 1:1). We often assume that "God" here refers to the Father. But according to the doctrine of inseparable operations (and Scripture), this action is carried out by the one God, not just one of the persons of God. At the same time, we want to recognize that God always acts *as triune*, because that is who he is. So we also want to say that each person of God creates. We can affirm both of these via the doctrine of appropriations and via reference to *taxis*, or "order." A common way to put it throughout church history is that the acts of God are *from* the Father, *through* the Son, and *by* the Spirit. So for the doctrine of creation, we can say that creation is from the Father, through the Son, and by the Spirit. Indeed, the Bible describes creation in this way. For example, Genesis 1:1–3 teaches that God spoke the world into existence with the Spirit of God hovering over the face of the waters. In a clear recapitulation of this creation narrative, John's Gospel asserts: "In the beginning was the Word, and the Word was with God, and the Word was God. He was in the beginning with God. All things were made through him, and without him was not any thing made that was made. In him was life, and the life was the light of men" (John 1:1–4). Later, Jesus says that it is the Spirit who gives life (John 6:63). Who gives life? The Father? Yes. The Son? Yes. The Spirit? Yes. Paul says similarly, "Yet for us there is one God, the Father, from whom are all things and for whom we exist, and one Lord, Jesus Christ, through whom are all things and through whom we exist" (1 Cor. 8:6).

To be specific, then, creation is from the Father in the sense that the Father speaks creation into existence. Creation is through the Son in the sense that the Son is the Father's Word, the word that he speaks in order to bring creation into existence. And creation is by the Spirit in the sense that it is the Spirit who actively carries out and brings to pass the Father's Word that he speaks on each day. Creation is from the Father, through the Son, and by the Spirit. So we see here that even when we say "God created all things," the Bible pressures us to recognize that we cannot say "God" without the Trinity.

We could multiply examples of this kind of talk, but we'll save it for the subsequent chapters, each of which discusses how God acts in a particular event in creation and redemption. For now, what's important is for us to recognize that any time we speak of an act of God, we have to maintain both his *oneness* and his *threeness* when we do so.

Where We're Going

In the following chapters, we aim to bring the idea of inseparable operations to bear on the most important doctrines of Scripture. While these concepts can be difficult to understand, they are crucial to understanding how our triune God has revealed himself to us. And after you read this book, our hope and prayer is that you will see the beauty of the Apostles' Creed like millennia of Christians before us:

I believe in God, the Father almighty,
 creator of heaven and earth.
I believe in Jesus Christ, his only Son, our Lord,
 who was conceived by the Spirit
 and born of the virgin Mary.
 He suffered under Pontius Pilate,
 was crucified, died, and was buried;
 he descended to hell.
 The third day he rose again from the dead.
 He ascended to heaven
 and is seated at the right hand of God the Father almighty.
 From there he will come to judge the living and the dead.

I believe in the Holy Spirit,
    the holy catholic [or, universal] church,
    the communion of saints,
    the forgiveness of sins,
    the resurrection of the body,
    and the life everlasting. Amen.

1

Revelation

HUMANITY HAS LOVED the pursuit of knowledge since the very beginning, when Adam and Eve ate of the forbidden fruit under the false impression that they should (or even could) know the things God knows (Gen. 3:5). What Adam and Eve should have accepted—and what humanity continues to need to accept—is, "The secret things belong to the LORD our God, but the things that are revealed belong to us and to our children forever, that we may do all the words of this law" (Deut. 29:29). Adam and Eve thought that God was holding out on them. They were duped by Satan into thinking that what God had already revealed wasn't enough and that they needed to get behind the curtain to find the good stuff. In this chapter, we hope to show that the triune God's self-revelation is not exhaustive but is completely sufficient for us and our salvation (now, that's the good stuff).

The doctrine of revelation seems simple enough: it describes the way in which God reveals knowledge of himself and his salvific will to humankind. This definition is true enough but, as we will see, the biblical description of God's revelation of himself is much richer and more beautiful than this. Scott Swain has helpfully argued that one way to think about God's revelation or self-communication is to situate it within a "trinitarian, covenantal context."[1] Put another way, the triune God's communication of himself reveals both something about his perfect being and life (*ad intra*) and something about his redemptive work in creation for us and our salvation (*ad extra*).

Trinitarian Unity in Revelation

The triune God's self-communication is entirely gratuitous—he didn't have to do it—and yet entirely consistent with his character—he created us to know and be in communion with him. Athanasius of Alexandria makes this argument beautifully in *On the Incarnation*. As Athanasius sees it, Adam and Eve's sin creates a "divine dilemma." On the one hand, God created mankind to know him. On the other hand, God promised to punish them if they sinned. And when they sinned, they turned their eyes away from God and toward idolatry of creation, making it impossible for them to save themselves. Athanasius then asks the important question: in light of their sin and its consequences, what was God to do?

> So the Word of God came himself, in order that he being the image of the Father (cf. Col. 1.15), the human being "in the image" might be recreated. It could not, again, have been done in any other way, without death and corruption being utterly

1 Scott R. Swain, *Trinity, Reading, and Revelation: A Theological Introduction to the Bible and Its Interpretation* (London: T&T Clark, 2011), 7.

destroyed. So he rightly took a mortal body, that in it death might henceforth be destroyed utterly and human beings be renewed again according to the image. For this purpose, then, there was need of none other than the Image of the Father.[2]

God is not a liar and so there would be consequences for their sin. That much seems obvious. But did God *have to* redeem Adam and Eve? Certainly not, insofar as God is lacking nothing (Acts 17:25). However, again, God is not a liar—he created humanity so that they would know him. So, then, it is entirely consistent with his character to redeem their knowledge and turn their eyes back toward him. Satan and sin would not have the last word. No, God himself would enter into his creation through the incarnation of the Son, the climax of revelation in biblical (and human) history. In the mission of the Son, God himself would stand in front of humanity to lift their eyes off of created things and back to beholding their Creator, restoring his image bearers to relationship with him through the incarnation of the Son, the true image (Heb. 1:3). The biblical storyline gestures toward this end both before and after Adam and Eve sinned.

God communicated and was present with his creation from the start. After all, the singular act of creation is a triune act: God spoke all things into existence by his Word and by the presence of his Spirit (Gen. 1:1–3ff.; Job 33:4; John 1:1–5). God spoke when he commanded Adam and Eve to multiply and to steward creation (Gen. 1:26–28). He spoke again when he called out to them after they sinned, once again commanding them to multiply and to

---

2 *On the Incarnation*, 13. English translation from Saint Athanasius, *On the Incarnation*, trans. John Behr (Yonkers, NY: SVS Press, 2011), 63.

steward creation even through the frustration of sin's consequences (Gen. 3:9–20). God showed immediately that he was still with his people, revealing who he is and keeping his covenantal promise to know and be known by his people.[3]

As the biblical storyline unfolds, this covenantal self-communication continues. The book of Exodus, for example, is one long story of God's presence among his people, revealing who he is and who he commands them to be. Starting with Moses's encounter with the burning bush (Ex. 3) and continuing through the Israelites' wandering in the wilderness, God's presence is evident, but he is veiled by smoke, clouds, or fire. The famous story of the golden calf—in which the Israelites create an idol to worship as a response to impatience for God's revelation (Ex. 32:1–6)—reminds us that, much like Adam and Eve, God's people wanted more. And if we're thinking along the lines of Athanasius above, we may also wonder why God desires to be known and yet veils himself. There are at least two reasons worth considering.

First, we are sinners. Sin hampers our ability to know God and to behold his glory because we, like Adam and Eve and the Israelites, "suppress the truth" (Rom. 1:18). We often don't even *want to* know and behold the Lord. Second, and more foundationally, we are creatures. Even before they sinned, we should remember that Adam and Eve were still finite creatures. They still relied on their Creator for sustenance and wisdom. The Creator/creature

---

3 Though scholars have spilt much ink debating what constitutes a covenant and whether there is such a thing as either an eternal "covenant of redemption" between the divine persons or an Adamic or Edenic covenant between God and humanity, we are using the term more broadly to describe the self-giving binding of God to his people and his people to him. We rely again on Swain, *Trinity, Reading, and Revelation*, 18–19, for this general definition.

distinction exists because the triune God is eternal and infinite; even sinless humans were (and will be in the new creation) temporal and finite. The church has classically called this God's "incomprehensibility" or "divine otherness": that God can be known as he has revealed himself, but nonetheless he is utterly distinct from us as the eternal sovereign God of the universe. As such, he cannot be fully comprehended as though he is a subject in a textbook or petri dish that can be fully examined and explained. But, again, this doesn't mean that he is *unknowable*.

Consider a well-known scene from Exodus 33. After several trips to speak with the Lord, Moses finally pleads for an unveiled glimpse at his glory:

> Moses said, "Please show me your glory." And [the Lord] said, "I will make all my goodness pass before you and will proclaim before you my name 'The LORD.' And I will be gracious to whom I will be gracious, and will show mercy on whom I will show mercy. But," he said, "you cannot see my face, for man shall not see me and live." And the LORD said, "Behold, there is a place by me where you shall stand on the rock, and while my glory passes by I will put you in a cleft of the rock, and I will cover you with my hand until I have passed by. Then I will take away my hand, and you shall see my back, but my face shall not be seen." (33:18–23)

Notice here that God doesn't reject Moses's request. He wants to be known—he has proven this consistently already. He has told his people his name, articulates his will and his response to his people's obedience/disobedience, and even allows Moses a tangible glimpse of him passing by the cleft. At the same time, Moses cannot look directly at God's "face" and live. Because God is spirit and noncorporeal (John 4:24; 1 Tim. 1:17), "face" here likely means something like an ability to fully comprehend one's identity or even essence, not a literal physical face with eyes, nose, and mouth.

As the biblical storyline continues, God's veiled presence continues in the form of the tabernacle and the temple, and through various other mediatory modes like speaking through angels and prophets. This veiled presence is the paradox we must accept in the triune God's self-communication to his people. He wants to be known and makes himself known, albeit in a way that accommodates finite humanity. In the transition from the Old Testament to the New, the divine missions further bring God's promises to bear.

Trinitarian Distinction in Revelation

The one God of Israel is the triune God who communicates and covenants with his people. There was always a foreshadowing in the Hebrew Scriptures that this one God included the identities of a Father (Ex. 4:22; Isa. 63:16), a Son (Pss. 2:7–12; 110:1–3; Isa. 7:14), and a Holy Spirit (Neh. 9:20; Isa. 32:15; Joel 2:28–32).[4] The earliest Christians were good readers of Scripture, and when they encountered the person and work of Jesus and the Holy Spirit, they were pressured to see the one God of Israel as Father, Son, and Holy Spirit (Matt. 1:21–23; 22:43; John 1:1–3; 14:26–15:26; Acts 2:16–21).[5]

---

4   These references are obviously nowhere near comprehensive but are rather representative.

5   There are various ways to describe how the Old Testament's revelation of God relates to the doctrine of the Trinity. For a few helpful proposals, see C. Kavin Rowe, "Biblical

More specifically, *inseparable operations* is a category that helps us affirm that the one God of Israel who self-communicated and covenanted with his people in the Old Testament *just is* the one God who is Father, Son, and Holy Spirit. We mentioned at the outset of this chapter that the triune God's communication of himself reveals both something about his perfect being and life (*ad intra*) and something about his redemptive work in creation for us and our salvation (*ad extra*). Put another way, we know *who* God is in large part by what he *says* and *does*. We can now reflect on this statement in more detail as it relates to revelation.

As we explained at the beginning of this book, it's best to speak about the eternal triune life *ad intra* (or, "toward the inside") in terms of *eternal relations* and *processions*. While not using the terms explicitly, the Bible teaches these eternal relations by explaining how Father, Son, and Holy Spirit have lived in perfect relation to one another before the foundation of the world. Consider once again Genesis 1, where the Father speaks his Word by the presence of his Spirit—all three persons act inseparably in the act of creation, showing their eternal unity and distinction as the Creator. Or consider John 17, in which Jesus prays that his disciples will love one another just as he and the Father loved one another "before the foundation of the world" (v. 24). This is once again language about their eternal relations: they are the Father and the Son who have shared this bond of love since before time

Pressure and Trinitarian Hermeneutics," *Pro Ecclesia* 11/3 (2002): 295–312; Fred Sanders, *The Triune God* (Grand Rapids, MI: Zondervan Academic, 2016), 209–37; Christopher R. Seitz, *The Elder Testament: Canon, Theology, Trinity* (Waco, TX: Baylor University, 2018); Heath A. Thomas, "Old Testament," in *The Trinity in the Canon: A Biblical, Theological, Historical, and Practical Proposal*, ed. Brandon D. Smith (Nashville, TN: B&H Academic, 2023), 61–82.

began.[6] As Baptist theologian John Gill said, "Whatever distinguishes them cannot arise from, nor depend upon any works done by them in time, since their distinction is from eternity."[7] The Son eternally proceeds from the Father by generation; the Spirit eternally proceeds from the Father and Son by spiration ("breathing").

These eternal relations or processions are most clearly revealed *ad extra* ("toward the outside") in the divine *missions*: the sending of the Son (incarnation) and the Spirit (Pentecost). So when we talk about God's revelation—specifically his communication and covenant with his people—the divine missions are ultimately at the center. Why? Because these missions are the further unveiling of God's purposes to know and redeem his people that have already been mentioned in the Old Testament. They are not merely gesturing toward or beginning to unveil the mystery of the Trinity as though we're waiting for something else in the future; they are specific manifestations of the divine persons in creation for the sake of revelation. When Jesus said, "Do not think that I have come to abolish the Law or the Prophets; I have not come to abolish them but to fulfill them" (Matt. 5:17) or, "Everything written about me in the Law of Moses and the Prophets and the Psalms must be fulfilled" (Luke 24:44), we should recognize that

---

6 Pushing further, many have argued throughout church history that this bond of love or communion is the Holy Spirit, citing especially the Spirit's work as a comforter and unifier of God's people in Jesus's discourse in John 14–17 or Paul's reasoning in 1 Cor. 12–13 and Eph. 4:3–4, though our argument doesn't depend on affirming this. Augustine of Hippo's *On the Trinity* is most notable for introducing this idea to the church more broadly in, e.g., 5.3.12.

7 John Gill, *A Complete Body of Doctrinal and Practical Divinity* (Paris, AR: Baptist Standard Bearer, 2007), 1.28.2.

the incarnation is an act of revelation. It would be fair to say that the incarnation is the climax of history, but we should be careful not to say that this is something *entirely* new—as we have seen, the whole biblical storyline leading up to this moment has portrayed God as present with his people, revealing who he is and what he commands of his people. The eternal Son who put on flesh was sent by the Father to reveal and further bring to bear his salvific love, and they sent the Holy Spirit to further reveal and bring to bear those salvific purposes (John 3:16; Eph. 3:3–14). Indeed, the Holy Spirit makes us "God's temple" (1 Cor. 3:16) and was sent so that the Father and the Son could dwell with us (John 14:23–26).

Scripture as God's Revelation

The content of revelation is God himself, and the one who enacts the revelation is that same God as an act of grace and mercy.[8] We see this throughout Scripture. Though we have already discussed the various ways God has revealed himself to his people and made himself present among them, a notable omission thus far has been God's revelation in Scripture. After all, Scripture has been the locus of authority for all of our claims thus far. But this point has been delayed because it depends on what we've said above.

Paul tells us, "All Scripture is breathed out by God and profitable for teaching, for reproof, for correction, and for training in righteousness, that the man of God may be complete, equipped for every good work" (2 Tim. 3:16–17). How do we know that

---

8 John Webster, *Holy Scripture: A Dogmatic Sketch* (Cambridge, UK: Cambridge University Press, 2003), 14.

God has revealed himself to us and intends to know us? By reading Scripture as people united with Christ and indwelled by the Holy Spirit. Scripture—God's final revelation to his people—sums up, describes, and brings forth all other revelatory acts beforehand. God's very words have always been a significant part of the life of God's people—from creation to communication to covenant—and the Scriptures were being written, taught, and shared to preserve his words. This is why prophets, priests, and kings were all bound by Scripture (Deut. 17:18–20; Neh. 8:1–3; Isa. 36:14), and why Peter defended the authority of both the Old Testament and Paul's letters even as the New Testament was being formed (2 Pet. 1:21; 3:16). Both Paul and Peter also affirm that the Scriptures were inspired by the Holy Spirit, who, as we mentioned above, was sent by the Father and the Son to bring God's promises to bear.

For most of Christian history, Scripture as God's revelation was always tied to the revelatory acts of God throughout human history, particularly the revelatory work of the Son (incarnation) and the Spirit (inspiration and illumination). We already saw above the way Athanasius articulates the relationship between revelation and the incarnation of the Son. Now, let's consider this quote by John Calvin regarding the relationship between revelation, Scripture, and the Holy Spirit:

> The testimony of the Spirit is more excellent than all reason. For as God alone is a fit witness of himself in his Word, so also the Word will not find acceptance in men's hearts before it is sealed by the inward testimony of the Spirit. The same Spirit, therefore, who has spoken through the mouths of the prophets

must penetrate into our hearts to persuade us that they faithfully proclaimed what had been divinely commanded.[9]

Calvin reinforces what we said above: revelation ultimately has God as its content and originator. Therefore, whether we are speaking of Moses on the mountain or any one of us reading Scripture today, God's work is required for us to truly know him and be redeemed by him. The missions of the Son and the Spirit give us post–New Testament readers the ability to know God, gain wisdom from him, and live according to his ways (1 Cor. 2). *That same Word*, the Son, speaks to us through the Scriptures by *that same Spirit* who inspired those who wrote them. Our triune God wants to know us and be known by us—he's proven it since the moment he said, "Let there be . . ."

Ultimately, then, revelation has a Trinitarian shape. The incarnate Son is the image of the invisible God (Col. 1:15), the radiance of the glory of God and the exact imprint of his nature (Heb. 1:2), and the one in whom we see the Father (John 14:9–10). And it is the Spirit who testifies to the Son (John 15:26–27; 16:13–15; 2 Cor. 3:17–18). Through the Spirit's testimony, climactically through the incarnate Son and through the Scriptures which testify to him (Luke 24:27, 44; John 5:46; 1 Pet. 1:10–12), we see the Son in whom we know the Father. The Trinitarian shape of revelation explains Trinitarian distinction in revelation. It is the Son who becomes incarnate by the agency of the Holy Spirit so that, in the Son, we can see the Father. It is the Spirit who testifies to the Son in the

9 John Calvin, *Institutes of the Christian Religion*, ed. John T. McNeill, trans. Ford Lewis Battles (Louisville, KY: Westminster John Knox Press, 1960), 1.7.4.

incarnation and in inspiration because it is in seeing the Son that we see the Father.

Beholding the Triune God in Revelation

To behold is to see or observe. There is perhaps no clearer way to describe the way we behold our triune God than through his self-revelation. The other doctrines in this book flow from this one, for we would not be able to speak any further about God's being and actions without him first making himself known to us in creation and salvation.

There are times in any Christian's life when we feel like God is silent, that our prayers hit the ceiling and go no further. But God has told and shown us clearly that this is not the case. No, our triune God wants us to know him. He's gratuitously and lavishly given us everything we need for salvation, for a redemption of our knowledge of him, so that we might know, love, and follow him.

2

Providence

FOR MILLENNIA, Christians have debated exactly what God's providence entails. Does providence mean that God micromanages every single subatomic particle across all of time and space? Does providence mean that God's sovereignty overpowers humanity's "free" will, such that we don't really make our own decisions? What about all the suffering and calamity in the world—does God actually have little control over creation or, worse, does he simply not care? Is creation like a clock that has been wound up, set into motion, and then left behind such that the providence of God is relatively inconsequential? These are all legitimate questions that we cannot fully answer in this chapter (or, if we're honest, this side of eternity), but are nonetheless the types of questions that will inevitably arise when thinking about the Trinity and providence.

Here is a simple definition for God's providence that would satisfy most Christians: God's providence is both his eternal, perfect knowledge of all things and his active, ongoing activity in and authority over creation. The doctrine of providence pervades all other doctrines we will cover in this book, in the sense that providence speaks to God's creation of all things, his salvation of sinners, and his carrying of all things to their intended end. Second-century theologian Irenaeus of Lyons put it this way:

> God does, however, exercise a providence over all things, and therefore he also gives counsel; and when giving counsel, he is present with those who attend to moral discipline. It follows then of course, that the things which are watched over and governed should be acquainted with their ruler; which things are not irrational or vain, but they have understanding derived from the providence of God.[1]

Irenaeus helpfully explains here that God's providence is both a fact and a source of wisdom: he is over all things, but also a type of counsel and understanding for those who draw near to his presence.

God's providence serves as a means of comfort for us sinners living in a broken world, often wondering if God sees our tears and hears our cries. Scripture says, simply, that God does indeed see and hear, so much so that he's promised to wipe away every tear and end all mourning in the new creation (Rev. 21:4). This is a promise he made to our first parents when they introduced sin into the world (Gen. 3:15). And because the Christian doctrine of God just is the doctrine of the Trinity, God's providence is no

---

1 Irenaeus of Lyons, *Against Heresies* 3.25.1. English translation from *Irenaeus: Essential Readings*, ed. Ched Spellman (Dallas, TX: Fontes Press, 2023).

providential work of God that is not a singular and indivisible act of Father, Son, and Spirit.

Trinitarian Unity in Providence

God's providence is so evident in his creation and to his creatures that Paul can say:

> For the wrath of God is revealed from heaven against all ungodliness and unrighteousness of men, who by their unrighteousness suppress the truth. For what can be known about God is plain to them, because God has shown it to them. For his invisible attributes, namely, his eternal power and divine nature, have been clearly perceived, ever since the creation of the world, in the things that have been made. So they are without excuse. (Rom. 1:18–20)

If someone denies the existence of God, Paul asserts that it's not due to God's hiddenness, but rather to one's own sinful willingness to "suppress the truth." If it's true that "the heavens declare the glory of God, and the sky above proclaims his handiwork" (Ps. 19:1), then we can know without a doubt that God has not merely created all things at some time in the past but that his providential work in the creation and his intent to know his people is an ongoing activity.

To this end, we can describe the triune God's providence in relation to at least four primary activities. First, as mentioned above, God's providence is related to his *knowledge* of creation and creatures. The overarching scope of God's dealings with creation is related to his supreme, perfect, and unbounded knowledge of all things. Before the foundation of the world, Peter says, the eternal Son knew that he would come to be "made manifest" for us and our salvation (1 Pet. 1:20). Indeed, the incarnation is inseparable from both the Father's "foreknowledge" and "definite plan" and the Spirit's anticipated pouring out to apply and seal this covenantal work of the triune God (Acts 2:16–23; Eph. 1:3–14). This divine knowledge is held by Father, Son, and Spirit equally and without confusion or contradiction. The Son was not surprised by his being sent by the Father, nor was the Spirit surprised by his being sent by the Father and the Son. Not only did God promise this through prophets such as Ezekiel and Joel (Ezek. 36:26; Joel 2:28–32), but Jesus reiterated the promise in John 15:26: "When the Helper comes, whom I will send to you from the Father, the Spirit of truth, who proceeds from the Father, he will bear witness about me."[2] God's providential knowledge is a knowledge belonging to Father, Son, and Spirit and revealed to us by Father, Son, and Spirit (1 Cor. 2).

Second, God's providence is related to his *presence* in creation and the lives of his creatures. In the beginning, God didn't merely wind up the clock of creation, as it were, and send off creation to fend for itself. Rather, Scripture says that the Spirit "was hovering over the face of the waters" as the very presence of God right in the midst of his creation as he providentially ordered all things (Gen. 1:2). Then God began speaking all things into existence, and, as John says, this Word was the Son through whom "all things were made" (John 1:1–3). This creative work reached its pinnacle with the creation of his image bearers, Adam and Eve.

---

2 This promise of the Spirit's coming is littered throughout John's Gospel and especially in chaps. 14–16.

The triune God demonstrated once again that he was present in creation (Spirit) by speaking to them (Word) and giving them the command to "be fruitful and multiply and fill the earth and subdue it, and have dominion over the fish of the sea and over the birds of the heavens and over every living thing that moves on the earth" (Gen. 1:26–28). As the story of Scripture unfolds, the reader will notice that the triune God continues to speak and draw near to his people at every turn.

Third, God's providence is related to his *provision* for his creation and creatures. Whether or not one holds a strong view of God's micromanagement of every subatomic particle in creation, Scripture clearly teaches that God is not just the initial cause of creation, but also the one who continually sustains it. The Father provides for his creation, from the birds of the air to the lilies of the field, and especially he provides for his people (Matt. 6:25–26; James 1:17). The Son is the one through whom "all things were created" and who "upholds the universe by the word of his power" (Col. 1:16–17; Heb. 1:2–3). The Spirit sustains all of creation as the continual presence of God at creation all the way through his eternal life-giving work in the new Jerusalem as the river of life that flows from the throne of God and the Lamb (Gen. 1:2; Rev. 22:1–2; cf. John 4:14; 7:37–39). The triune God providentially provides for his creation and his creatures through his generous grace and his upholding of all things.

Fourth, God's providence is related to his *completion* of his purposes for creation and his creatures. Again, Revelation 21–22 tells us that God's promise of redemption would finally come true. This culmination of humanity's long anticipation of redemption is a triune act; new creation brings forth the Father's foreordained plan of salvation, the Son's accomplishment of this salvation, and the Spirit's application of this salvation. In the new creation, the throne of God at the center of the new Jerusalem is occupied by the Father and the Son, who send the Spirit as a life-giving river of life to all who will drink from it for eternity (Rev. 22:1–2). Paul is so confident in God's providence and fulfillment of his promises that he encourages the Philippians, "He who began a good work in you will bring it to completion at the day of Jesus Christ" (Phil. 1:6).

The triune God always acts with one will, power, and authority. The doctrine of providence is a beautiful reminder of God's power and perfection—the promises of God are sure because the same God who promised a redeemer has thus far sovereignly carried the redemption story forward toward its proper end. Indeed, the unfolding of salvation history in Scripture is the clearest example of the triune God's providence. The Father, the Son, and the Spirit inseparably and with one will, power, and authority know all things, created all things, sustain all things, and will complete his redemption of all things. We will now survey the distinction of the persons in God's providence to highlight how Scripture's emphasis on their unity is still bound up with a distinction of persons.

Trinitarian Distinction in Providence

The Father's desire to offer a salvific inheritance to his children is on clear display in his sending of the Son and the Spirit. When we speak of the Father as the sender of the Son and the Spirit, we are not speaking of a hierarchy among the persons of the Trinity. Father, Son, and Spirit are each truly and fully God, therefore they each possess the full measure of divine authority and power. The doctrine of inseparable operations is a category that helps us avoid the mistake of ranking the persons; instead, it helps us affirm Scripture's dual affirmation of God's unity in essence and distinction in personhood. In short, then, the Son's and the Spirit's missions in salvation history further teach us about the providence of God, because the Son and the Spirit, being God, are God's providential presence in creation and the fulfillment of his promises of redemption.

One noticeable aspect of God's providence in Scripture is the forward-pointing prophecies and promises. When God makes his covenant with David and promises a future for his throne, David models faith in God's providence: "O Lord God, you are God, and your words are true, and you have promised this good thing to your servant. . . . For you, O Lord God, have spoken, and with your blessing shall the house of your servant be blessed forever" (2 Sam. 7:28–29). David fully expected the promise to come true. Why? Because God does not lie, God is not bound by time and space, and God's will cannot be thwarted. There are numerous promises just like this throughout all of the Old Testament. And when God's people were tempted to wonder if God would ever make good on these promises, they are reminded that God was with them in Egypt and the wilderness and exile, and he would be with them to the end (Ps. 136; Jer. 29:14).

All of God's promises were not devoid of the Son and the Spirit, as though the "God of the Old Testament" is merely the Father. The Word of God and the Spirit of God were always at work and always guiding God's people. But the Word and the Spirit are not merely extensions of the Father or "parts" of him. We know this because the identities of the Word and the Spirit are fully revealed as divine persons in the incarnation and Pentecost.

Likewise, Peter tells us that the Spirit was always at work not just as the presence of God among his people, but as the one who inspired the prophets to speak God's words (2 Pet. 1:21) and who continues to "guide [his people] into all the truth" by teaching and reminding us of the Father and the Son's words (John 16:13). And the fulfillment of these promises, the new covenant inaugurated by the Son and sealed by the Spirit, emphasizes that this is the triune God's providence at work. From Genesis to Revelation, there is simply no work of God's providence that doesn't include Father, Son, and Spirit.

Mark's Gospel opens with a word for the anticipation of God's people:

The beginning of the gospel of Jesus Christ, the Son of God. As it is written in Isaiah the prophet,

"Behold, I send my messenger before your face,
    who will prepare your way,
the voice of one crying in the wilderness:
    'Prepare the way of the Lord,
    make his paths straight.'" (Mark 1:1–3; cf. Isa. 40:3)

John the Baptist fulfilled this promise of being a messenger for the Messiah, crying out in the wilderness for people to repent and be baptized for the forgiveness of sins. John's Gospel tells us exactly who this Messiah is: the Word of God who is God and is with God, and who put on flesh and dwelt among us (John 1:1, 14). He is the God who promised and still promises to save, and the man who would come to crush the serpent's head and inaugurate a new covenant.

The image of God the Father as *our* Father hits us powerfully when we think of his providence (Matt. 6:9). Our perfect and good Father in heaven knows us, is with us, provides for us, and keeps his promises. And he does this through the sending of his very own Son, who with the Father wills and works for us and our salvation. Indeed, the providence of God is spotlighted in the missions of the Son (incarnation) and the Spirit (Pentecost). In the incarnation of the Son, God's foreknowledge and promises are fulfilled; God is present among his people; God offers provision and sustenance; and we see the beginning of the culmination of God's promises. He is God in the flesh, the providence of God with ten fingers and ten toes. He became truly human to make us truly human again. Athanasius of Alexandria put it plainly: "Being the Word of the Father and above all, he alone consequently was both able to recreate the universe and was worthy to suffer on behalf of all and to intercede for all before the Father."[3] The incarnation is not a sign that the Son of God somehow lost his divine power to save; rather, the incarnation shows the extent to which God is willing and able to continue his providential project of new creation.

In the pouring out of the Spirit at Pentecost, we also see the providence of God in the same ways: God's foreknowledge and promises are fulfilled; God is present among his people; God offers provision and sustenance; and we see the beginning of the culmination of God's promises. He is God's indwelling presence, the providence of God living in us and making us his temples (1 Cor. 3:16). The indwelling of the Spirit also means that the

3   Athanasius of Alexandria, *On the Incarnation*, trans. John Behr (Yonkers, NY: SVS Press, 2011), 56.

Father and the Son have made their home with us (John 14:23). This is a good reminder that anytime Scripture speaks of the persons in distinction, there is an accompanying implication of their unity.

God's providence is evident in the fact that this triune indwelling has immediate effects—because "the kingdom of heaven is at hand," we know that "if anyone is in Christ, he is a new creation" (Matt. 3:2; 2 Cor. 5:17). Christians are, right now, already living in the Trinitarian work of new creation as we await final redemption. We are sons and daughters of the Father, coheirs with the Son, and guaranteed our future inheritance through the Spirit.

New Creation and the Trinity

New creation has made a few appearances in this chapter thus far, and it's worth drawing out more implications about God's providence in the book of Revelation. Revelation is more than the last book in Scripture's table of contents—it serves as the capstone to and fulfillment of the biblical storyline. This dynamic is most obvious due to the quotes and allusions from the Old Testament, showing how the book culminates in all of those prophecies and promises coming true.

Revelation is an apocalyptic letter with the explicit purpose of telling the church that Jesus is coming soon (Rev. 22:12). This communicates to the first-century church and the church today that while God has not yet made all things new, he is still *making* all things new in his providential sovereignty over history. There is no doubt that Isaiah's consolation, "They who wait for the LORD shall renew their strength," is a promise the triune God will make good on (Isa. 40:31). This is especially comforting to the church who, for two millennia, has held on to these promises and found peace and joy, even in the midst of war, plague, death, and injustice.

In the opening chapter, John tells us that God has a word of grace and peace for his audience—a triune blessing from "him who is and who was and who is to come [the Father], and from the seven spirits who are before his throne [the Holy Spirit], and from Jesus Christ the faithful witness, the firstborn of the dead, and the ruler of kings on earth" (Rev. 1:4–5).[4] All who hear this word are, along with John, brothers and partners "in the tribulation and the kingdom and the patient endurance that are in Jesus" (1:9). They are all longing for new creation, and "the revelation of Jesus Christ, which God gave him to show to his servants" (1:1), offers a resolution for that longing.

The Father's knowledge and enacting of his own providential plan for history is unveiled in the revelation of Jesus Christ, the Word made flesh, through John's visions "in the Spirit" (1:1, 10). The various churches of Revelation 2–3 all hear a word from Jesus about their good and bad works, being warned at the end of each message to "hear what the Spirit says to the churches" so that they might be found faithful when he returns (e.g., 2:7). Straight away, the whole book of Revelation is ordered in terms of the indivisible providence of the triune God; there is no fulfillment of God's providential plan of redemption—and no revealing of it to us— apart from the inseparable operations of Father, Son, and Spirit.

When John is ushered into the throne room by the Spirit, he receives a stunning vision of the throne room of God, where he

---

4 For a fuller treatment of the Trinity in Revelation, see Brandon D. Smith, *The Trinity in the Book of Revelation: Seeing Father, Son, and Holy Spirit in John's Apocalypse* (Downers Grove, IL: IVP Academic, 2022).

sees the Father and the Son sharing the divine throne and receiving worship from all of creation (4:8–11; 5:12–14; 7:15–17; 22:3), as well as the Spirit being sent out from the throne into the earth as the eyes of the Lamb (5:6). All of creation faces the throne, worshiping the triune God as creator and sustainer of all things; Father, Son, and Spirit are on the "throne side" of the heavenly topography, receiving praise and working indivisibly to bring about new creation.

Through the twists and turns of Revelation's spellbinding series of events, the promise of new creation reaches its conclusion at the return of Christ, the divine Lamb and King. In Revelation 19, those around the throne are invited to the great "marriage supper of the Lamb" and witness the return of Christ, who is called "Faithful and True," "the Word of God," and the "King of kings and Lord of lords" (19:9, 11, 13, 16). The Word of God, the Creator of all things, the God who put on flesh and dwelt among us—he is coming back to continue the providential plan of God to complete the work of new creation. This redemptive work, starting in the incarnation and reaching its pinnacle in the second coming, includes the binding of Satan, the vindication of martyrs, and the Son's coheirs taking their seat as kings of creation under the throne of God (Rev. 20). Promise after promise, fulfilled by the triune God in the presence of his people.

Finally, Satan and the wicked are done away with once and for all as the offspring of Adam and Eve, the second Adam, crushes the serpent's head (20:14; cf. Gen. 3:15). Then the new heavens and the new earth, promised long ago in Isaiah 65:17–19, make their grand entrance into the final act of God's redemptive story. John, in the Spirit, hears the proclamation:

I heard a loud voice from the throne saying, "Behold, the dwelling place of God is with man. He will dwell with them, and they will be his people, and God himself will be with them as their God. He will wipe away every tear from their eyes, and death shall be no more, neither shall there be mourning, nor crying, nor pain anymore, for the former things have passed away." (Rev. 21:3–4)

Not only has the triune God's providential *foreknowledge* and *plan* come to fruition, not only is it clear that he has *sustained* and *provided* for creation every step of the way, not only has he *completed* his work, but at the center of the scene is his *presence*: God dwelling with man, where we will see him "face to face," as Paul promised (1 Cor. 13:12). The triune God has always been present—from the opening verses of Genesis, through the Old Testament storyline, and through the missions of the Son and the Spirit in the last days—but Revelation shows that in the new creation, his presence will be full and unincumbered.

The tree of life that Adam and Eve were ushered away from when they sinned is back in the middle of the new Jerusalem, once again signifying life with God (Gen. 3:22–24; Rev. 22:2). And, lest we forget, this life with God is life with the Trinity. God's people have unfettered access to "the throne of God and of the Lamb" and are given eternal life through the Spirit, "the river of the water of life" (Rev. 22:1). As we mentioned above, the Spirit's provision of eternal life as "water" matches promises of redemption and presence that God would providentially fulfill, starting with the promises of Joel 2:28–32 and Ezekiel 36:26, repeated by Jesus (John 3:8; 4:14; 7:37–39), and coming to fruition at Pentecost

(Acts 2). The Father sent the Son to become incarnate, and they sent the Spirit to indwell us—there is a clear distinction between them as divine persons—and yet God's providence cannot be described apart from the indivisible acts of the one God who is Father, Son, and Spirit.

Beholding the Triune God in Providence

The Father, the Son, and the Spirit are the one triune God, and thus have the same will, power, and authority to reign providentially over history. In the beginning and throughout history, God's Word and Spirit created, sustained, and were present among his creation as history moved toward his ordained culmination in new creation. In the missions of the Son and the Spirit as the sent ones, we see the providence of God "in action," as it were, through their triunity in their providential work in the world. We place our present and future hope in the Lord—Father, Son, and Spirit.

Jesus prepared his disciples—and us—with the promise that though we may not yet see him face-to-face, we can "behold" that he will be with us "to the end of the age" (Matt. 28:20). How do we behold him when our eyes can't lock onto his face? We can behold him through the Scriptures, as we see the words that we are called to hear (Rev. 2–3). We can behold him in "the peace of God, which surpasses all understanding," which will guard our hearts and our minds in Christ Jesus (Phil. 4:7). We can behold him in his creation, as "the heavens declare the glory of God" (Ps. 19:1). As we long for new creation, we can rest in the fact that through the Comforter, the indwelling Spirit, we are the temples of God in whom the Father and the Son have made their home (John 14:23–25; 1 Cor 3:16).

3

Creation

.

"I BELIEVE IN GOD the Father Almighty, creator of heaven and
earth"—the first article of the Apostles' Creed begins by appropriating the work of creation to God the Father. In the minds
of many of us, this is not mere appropriation but actually a full
account of God's work in creation; it is God the Father who is
the primary architect of the cosmos. While he involves the Son
and the Spirit, it is the Father who directs and guides this first
external work of God. But this kind of articulation of creation
poses the same problems to the doctrine of God that we worked
through in the introduction. The Father in this scenario is in
some sense in authority over the Son and the Spirit, placing ontological differentiation in the Godhead. It also would mean that
there are three "actors" in every act of God, thus gesturing toward
tritheism (three gods instead of one God). Aside from these very
serious theological problems, this articulation is also problematic
when we read the Bible carefully. In this chapter we will see that
while creation can be appropriated to the Father, it is ultimately

an inseparable work of the triune God, from the Father through the Son by the Spirit.

The doctrine of creation typically includes both the initial action of creation itself (i.e., Gen. 1–2) as well as God's ongoing work of sustaining creation, his status as the ongoing ruler of creation, and his providence over the actions of his creatures. The latter was discussed in the previous chapter. In this chapter, we will explore how the triune God acts inseparably in creation at its inception, in sustaining it, and in ruling over it. We will also see how it is appropriate to appropriate this work to God the Father.

Trinitarian Unity in Creation

Creation in Scripture is, in the most fundamental sense, the work of the Trinity. Many passages regarding creation in the Bible simply refer to it as the work of the one God without mention of any specific divine person. For instance in Job 38:4–7, the Lord asks Job:

> Where were you when I laid the foundation of the earth?
>> Tell me, if you have understanding.
> Who determined its measurements—surely you know!
>> Or who stretched the line upon it?
> On what were its bases sunk,
>> or who laid its cornerstone,
> when the morning stars sang together
>> and all the sons of God shouted for joy?

The answer, of course, is that the Lord, not Job, created the world and governs it. The psalms also emphasize the Lord's work of creation in, for instance, 8:3–4; 33:6; 74:12–17; and 104:5–9. The prophets, likewise, refer to God's act of and rule over creation in, for instance, Jeremiah 27:5 and Ezekiel 28.[1]

In short, then, we can ask, Who created the heavens and the earth? Based on Scripture, we would say the Lord, the one God of Israel. As Jeremiah says, "Ah, Lord GOD! It is you who have made the heavens and the earth by your great power and by your outstretched arm! Nothing is too hard for you" (Jer. 32:17). Other passages of Scripture, however, mention one or more of the divine persons specifically when they reference creation and thus emphasize the Trinitarian unity of God's act of creation. In that sense, then, we can also say that Father, Son, and Holy Spirit created the heavens and the earth.

We see this Trinitarian unity in this first of God's external acts in a number of passages throughout the Bible. The natural place to start is in the beginning, Genesis 1. In verse 1 we hear Moses say that "in the beginning, God [*Elohim*] created the heavens and the earth." Then, in the very next verse, Moses tells us that "the Spirit of God was hovering over the face of the waters" (1:2). And throughout the chapter, as God creates, he does so by speaking—creation happens through the Word of God. It is not exegetically naïve to say that Genesis 1 has a Trinitarian shape: from the Father through the Word (Son) by the Spirit.[2] As we will see, John 1 offers a retelling of the creation account with an emphasis on the creative Word as the Son.

---

1   We are indebted to John E. Anderson, "Creation," *Lexham Bible Dictionary* (Bellingham, WA: Lexham Press, 2016), for this pattern of biblical language and the specific Scripture references cited.

2   See Francis Watson, *Text, Church, and World: Biblical Interpretation in Theological Perspective* (Grand Rapids, MI: Eerdmans, 1994), 137–53.

A related passage is Proverbs 8:22–31. Here, the personified Lady Wisdom recounts creation, an act in which she was "possessed" by the Lord "at the beginning of his work, the first of his acts of old" (8:22). She then goes on to sing of her being "brought forth" by the Lord (8:24–26) before anything was made, and of her presence with God during his work of creation (8:27–29). The passage culminates with Lady Wisdom declaring that during creation,

> then I was beside him, like a master workman,
> and I was daily his delight,
>   rejoicing before him always,
> rejoicing in his inhabited world
>   and delighting in the children of man. (8:30–31)

While we do not have space to articulate all the reasons why, there is good reason to understand Lady Wisdom here as a figurative personification of God's wisdom. For example, Paul says that "Christ *is* the power of God and the wisdom of God" (1 Cor. 1:24 CSB).[3] Further, the relationship between wisdom as a person who creates and the Word as a person who creates is evident in John 1:1–3. Therefore the references in Proverbs to wisdom being "brought forth" and "possessed" prior to creation should be understood as references to the Son's eternal generation from the Father—that he is truly a Son and has always been a Son. And

---

3 For a recent attempt to explain the Christological interpretation of this passage, see Matthew Y. Emerson, "The Role of Proverbs 8: Eternal Generation and Hermeneutics Ancient and Modern," in *Retrieving Eternal Generation*, ed. Fred Sanders and Scott R. Swain (Grand Rapids, MI: Zondervan Academic, 2017), 44–66.

in reference to God's act of creation, this passage teaches that the Son, wisdom, was active in creation, along with the Father, as the Son who was with him for all eternity. Athanasius of Alexandria makes this point well:

> If He is Son, as the Father says, and the Scriptures proclaim, and "Son" is nothing else than what is generated from the Father; and what is generated from the Father is His Word (John 1:1–3), and Wisdom (1 Cor 1:24), and Radiance (Heb 1:3); what is to be said but that, in maintaining "Once the Son was not," they rob God of His Word, like plunderers, and openly predicate of Him that He was once without His proper Word and Wisdom, and that the Light was once without radiance, and the Fountain was once barren and dry?[4]

Put simply, if the Son is God's Word, wisdom, and radiance, then he must be an eternal Son who has always been with him. Otherwise there was a time when the Father was mute, dumb, and dull. The unchangeable God would have changed by adding attributes to himself or by becoming a Father in creating for himself a Son. But this wouldn't match the biblical account of God's simplicity and perfection. Therefore, the best conclusion is that the Father and the Son are involved in the one act of creation of the one God.

This is similar to what we find in New Testament accounts of creation, and especially to what we find in the prologue to John's

---

4 Athanasius, *Orations against the Arians* 1.14. English translation from *Nicene and Post-Nicene Fathers*, Second Series, vol. 4, ed. Philip Schaff and Henry Wace, trans. John Henry Newman and Archibald Robertson (Buffalo, NY: Christian Literature, 1892).

Gospel, which we have referenced several times already. The fourth Evangelist begins his story of Jesus by hearkening back to the beginning of all things:

> In the beginning was the Word, and the Word was with God, and the Word was God. He was in the beginning with God. All things were made through him, and without him was not any thing made that was made. (John 1:1–3)

Like wisdom in Proverbs 8, the Word is "with God" in the beginning, active in creation along "with God" (John 1:2). This is because God's wisdom and his Word are the same divine person, God the Son. And as in Proverbs 8, where wisdom is present for all of creation, so in John 1:3 it is through the Word that "all things were made," and "without him was not any thing made that was made."

The Synoptic Gospels also affirm Jesus's authority over creation (with the implication that he is creation's Creator) in a number of stories. The most prominent of these is the narrative of Jesus calming the storm (Mark 4:35–41; cf. Matt. 8:23–27; Luke 8:22–25). As James Edwards notes, this story echoes both certain psalms and Jonah 1, and for similar reasons. Only God can calm a storm like this, and only God can evoke the fear seen in both the sailors in Jonah 1 and the disciples in Mark 4. Their fear is a response to the obvious presence of God. Edwards says of this story and its Old Testament roots:

> In the OT God alone possesses power to quell natural storms such as this (Pss 65:7; 89:9; 104:7; also *T. Adam* 3:1). In this

story, Mark informs us that the same power and authority belong to Jesus. In a final allusion to the Jonah story in v. 41, Mark says that the disciples were terrified at the calming of the storm. Their exceeding fear repeats verbatim the fear of the sailors in the Jonah story (*ephobēthēsan phobon megan*, Jonah 1:10, 16). The pagan sailors in the Jonah story recognized God in the presence of the miracle and offered sacrifice to him. In the calming of the storm on the lake Jesus does again what only God can do (so 2:7–10), and Mark invites disciples, then and now, to recognize in Jesus the same presence of God.[5]

In other words, Jesus is in control of creation and even forces of nature that are hostile to humanity due to the effects of sin. And he is in control of creation because he is its Creator, as John 1:1–3 affirms.

Paul echoes this affirmation about the Son's activity and pre-eminence in creation in a few different passages. Perhaps most prominently, he says in Colossians 1:15–17:

He is the image of the invisible God, the firstborn of all creation. For by him all things were created, in heaven and on earth, visible and invisible, whether thrones or dominions or rulers or authorities—all things were created through him and for him. And he is before all things, and in him all things hold together.

The term "firstborn" does not mean "first of God's creations" here, but rather has the connotation of head or ruler, or even

---

5   James R. Edwards, *The Gospel according to Mark*, Pillar New Testament Commentary (Grand Rapids, MI: Eerdmans, 2002), 149.

pattern. We see this, for instance, in other places where firstborn language is used. Israel is called God's firstborn nation, though they're certainly not his first creations or first set of human beings (Ex. 4:22–23). One born first can lose firstborn privileges in the case of disobedience or even theft (Gen. 25:19–34; 35:23). God's covenant with David includes the appointment of the "firstborn" as a type of ruling status (Ps. 89:27).

So, then, "firstborn" does not require such a literal connotation that it *must mean* that the Son is created or came into existence at some place in time. The following verses in Colossians 1 also make this clear, as the Son surely cannot be both "the first of God's creations" and also the one by whom "*all things* were created" (v. 16). One would have to assert that "all things" means "all things *except one thing—the Son*." But since "in the beginning" in places like Genesis 1 and John 1 speaks more about the beginning of time and space, it also marks the beginning of things being created—and the Son is already there, the Word who is God and is with God. The Son is the one by whom all things are made, according to explicit passages in both John and Paul. Notice also that Paul affirms the continuing work of sustaining creation at the end of this phrase (Col. 1:17).

Another affirmation of the Son's activity in creation comes from Paul in 1 Corinthians 8:6, this time with a parallel phrase about the Father: "For us there is one God, the Father, from whom are all things and for whom we exist, and one Lord, Jesus Christ, through whom are all things and through whom we exist." In this verse Paul paraphrases the Shema (Deut. 6:4),[6] and also

6 For a good discussion of this point, see Wesley Hill, *Paul and the Trinity: Persons, Relations, and the Pauline Letters* (Grand Rapids, MI: Eerdmans, 2015).

appropriates creation—something only God does—both to the Father and the Son.

Two other New Testament texts are worth mentioning. First, in Hebrews 1 the author notes the Son's activity in creation in two different places. In verses 2–3, he says:

> He has spoken to us by his Son, whom he appointed the heir of all things, through whom also he created the world. He is the radiance of the glory of God and the exact imprint of his nature, and he upholds the universe by the word of his power.

Here, creation is from the Father "through" the Son (1:2), and is also upheld "by the word of" the Son's power (1:3). Later, in verses 10–12, quoting Psalm 102:25–27, the author argues that Scripture speaks of the Son thusly:

> You, Lord, laid the foundation of the earth in the beginning,
>   and the heavens are the work of your hands;
> they will perish, but you remain;
>   they will all wear out like a garment,
> like a robe you will roll them up,
>   like a garment they will be changed.
> But you are the same,
>   and your years will have no end.

Again, the Son is the one to whom creation is appropriated, since he is the one who "laid the foundation of the earth" (1:10).

Finally, in Revelation 3:14, Jesus addresses the church in Laodicea and refers to himself in the greeting as "the Amen, the faithful and true witness, the beginning of God's creation." The final phrase is similar to Colossians 1:15, in that both use terms that indicate Christ's rule over creation and his preeminence in it. While Paul uses πρωτότοκος (*prōtotokos*), "firstborn," and John uses ἀρχή (*archē*), "beginning," they both refer to the fact that Jesus is the head of creation. The implication, especially in Colossians 1:15 but also implicit throughout Revelation, is that Jesus is the head of creation because he is its Creator.

Throughout Scripture, then, we see that the triune God is the Creator of all things, and that he creates with a particular order, or *taxis*, from the Father through the Son by the Spirit. In the texts we have explored so far, the emphasis has been on this insepara-bility of divine operations in creation. Many texts in Scripture simply refer to creation as being from the triune God, without mentioning *taxis*, while others mention two or all three of the divine persons when they speak of this first of God's external acts. In this way, the Bible teaches that creation is an act carried out inseparably by all three divine persons.

Trinitarian Distinction in Creation

Did the Father create the heavens and the earth? Yes. Did the Son create the heavens and the earth? Yes. Did the Spirit create the heavens and the earth? Yes. Unlike some other doctrines covered in this book, such as salvation, Scripture does not offer such robust distinctions between the operations or missions of any particular divine person. We do see, however, that the three persons are all properly called the Creator of all things, each person specifically referenced in relation to creation, as we saw above.

And yet Scripture, as well as the Christian theological tradition, also appropriates creation specifically to God the Father. Interestingly, many of the texts above that mention one or more of the divine persons focus on the Son specifically. But there are at least two passages that are key to this appropriation to the Father. The first is Genesis 1. As we noted above, the framework of God's speech act, carried out in the agency of the Spirit, gives the text a Trinitarian shape. While we should not import Nicene language onto the Bible nor import New Testament language onto Moses's description, we can also confidently say that Moses authors this text in such a way that the plurality, and specifically the triunity, of the persons of the one God is inherent in this chapter both in shape of the act of creation and in specific language. Regarding the latter, we have already mentioned the distinction of "the Spirit of God" from "God" in verses 1–2, but we should also note that the term *Elohim* as well as the plural "Let us make" (Gen. 1:26) also give space for Trinitarian reflection and interpretation. Returning to the narrative repetitive framework, we see in Genesis 1 that creation is from the Father who speaks his Word, and that Word is made effective by the "Spirit of God," who "hover[s] over the face of the waters" in the beginning (Gen. 1:2). In this fundamental text regarding the event (and thus the doctrine) of creation, we see that it is appropriate to appropriate the work of creation to God the Father, even while recognizing it ultimately as an inseparable operation of the Holy Trinity.

This appropriation of creation to the Father is fitting according to Trinitarian *taxis*. In God's own life, he exists as one God in three persons, and the Father is, we could say, the fount of divinity. It is from the Father that the Son is eternally generated, and it is from the

Father and the Son that the Spirit proceeds. Thus, in the economy of creation and redemption, it is fitting—it fits the Trinity's existence *ad intra*—that the first of God's external acts is appropriated to the Father. Put another way, it makes sense to us that a good, loving Father creates and gives life to his children and that he can bless the world through his children (his Son and, by extension, his adopted sons and daughters) and his activity (his Spirit) (Eph. 1:3–14). This makes sense to us because when we see this in everyday human life, it's a faint picture of the way all of creation has been structured and patterned after the revelation and providence of the triune God. Creation is from the Father through the Son by the Spirit, as are all of God's acts, but this particular act as the beginning of God's work is appropriately appropriated to the Father, the one who can also be appropriately referred to as the first person of the Trinity, the one from whom the Son and the Spirit eternally receive the divine essence.

One Lord and Creator in the New Creation

Though we discussed new creation in the chapter on providence, it is worth returning to it here. Creation and new creation are obviously intertwined in God's plan of redemption, so we cannot avoid it here. For our purposes in this chapter, we will primarily note creation and new creation as an act of the triune God.

As we saw earlier, Paul in 1 Corinthians 8:6 applies the Shema of Deuteronomy 6:4 to both the Father and the Son. Whereas Deuteronomy 6:4 reads, "The LORD our God, the LORD is one" (*kyrios ho theos hemon kurios eis*), Paul splits the first phrase apart and applies both words that refer to Yahweh in Moses's speech to both the Father and the Son. "There is one God [*theos*], the Father," and "one Lord [*kyrios*], Jesus Christ." This one God, the God of Israel, is, according to Paul, the Father and the Son (and the Spirit, although he does not mention him in this specific text). And, as is true throughout Scripture, God and God alone is the one who creates the world. But Paul gives Trinitarian shape to God's act of creation in this verse, for it is "from" the Father that "all things" exist and it is "through" the Son that "all things" exist. Thus, 1 Corinthians 8:6 helps us with the inseparability of God's act of creation by saying that it is both the Father and the Son who create, and also with the shape of creation, which is from the Father and through the Son. Or, in the words of the doctrine of inseparable operations, creation is the work of the Trinity and also fittingly appropriated to God the Father.

Another example could be drawn from the hymns sung to the Father and the Son in Revelation. In Revelation 4:11, it appears the hymn is sung only to the Father as the Creator:

Worthy are you, our Lord and God,
    to receive glory and honor and power,
for you created all things,
        and by your will they existed and were created.

However, in Revelation 5:12–13, we see the Son ("the Lamb") sharing the throne with the Father and receiving hymnic worship:

"Worthy is the Lamb who was slain,
to receive power and wealth and wisdom and might
and honor and glory and blessing!" . . .

To him who sits on the throne and to the Lamb
be blessing and honor and glory and might forever and ever!

That same God who sits on the throne as the Creator of all things shares that same throne with his Son. Revelation 7 records one more hymn to the Father and the Son, which points to their inseparable work in the new creation:

> Therefore they are before the throne of God,
>> and serve him day and night in his temple;
>> and he who sits on the throne will shelter them with his
>>> presence.
> They shall hunger no more, neither thirst anymore;
>> the sun shall not strike them,
>> nor any scorching heat.
> For the Lamb in the midst of the throne will be their
>> shepherd,
>> and he will guide them to springs of living water,
> and God will wipe away every tear from their eyes.
>> (vv. 15–17)

The Father and Son are obviously on the throne and receiving worship as the sovereign Lord over all creation. The "living water" language here also matches new-creation language at the end of the book:

> Then the angel showed me the river of the water of life, bright as crystal, flowing from the throne of God and of the Lamb through the middle of the street of the city; also, on either side of the river, the tree of life with its twelve kinds of fruit, yielding its fruit each month. The leaves of the tree were for the healing of the nations. (22:1–2)

This living water, flowing from the throne of God and the Lamb, gives life to the new creation through its sustenance of the tree of life, just as the breath of God gave life to Adam and Eve, who partook from the tree of life themselves (Gen. 2). Considering the fact that God's "breath" and the "living water" are associated with the Spirit elsewhere, we also see the Spirit acting as the Creator and sustainer of the new creation (Job 33:4; John 4:14; 7:37–39; 20:22).

Beholding the Triune God in Creation

The work of creation is the work of the triune God. Throughout the Bible, this first of God's external acts is referred to as the work of the one God, and in some places specifically as the work of one or more of the divine persons. It is, as with all of God's acts, inseparably the work of the Trinity. But given the shape of Genesis 1 and the teaching of 1 Corinthians 8:6, it is fitting to appropriate God's initial external act to the Father specifically. And this biblical appropriation is also fitting according to Trinitarian *taxis*, or order—God's inner life is from the Father through the Son by the Spirit, and so it is fitting that God's external work is from the Father through the Son by the Spirit. Because creation is the first of God's external acts, it is appropriate to appropriate it to the Father specifically, the "fount of divinity" and the one from whom the Son and Spirit proceed eternally.

As we reflect on this chapter and those before it, we can be reminded of the goodness of knowing our triune God, who made us, knows us, and cares for us. By the Spirit, we can pray with all of creation in Revelation 4, "Worthy are you, our Lord and God, to receive glory and honor and power, for you created all things, and by your will they existed and were created" (v. 11). We can sing with all of creation in Revelation 5, "Worthy is the Lamb who was slain, to receive power and wealth and wisdom and might and honor and glory and blessing!" (v. 11). We can rest with all creation in the truth of Revelation 7, "For the Lamb in the midst of the throne will be their shepherd, and he will guide them to springs of living water, and God will wipe away every tear from their eyes" (v. 17). The triune God who created us will keep his promise to re-create us and all of creation. Because of who God is and how he has worked in history and in us today, we hold tight to these promises until Christ returns.

4

Salvation

"SALVATION BELONGS TO THE LORD," says Psalm 3:8, and the Bible presents the Lord ultimately as one God in three persons. The baptismal formula of Matthew 28:19 ties together a Trinitarian shape to salvation and worship: Jesus commands us to baptize disciples in "the name [singular] of the Father and of the Son and of the Spirit [plural]." So when we discuss salvation, we cannot merely stop at Jesus's incarnate work in the cross and resurrection, for example; instead, we must discuss the unity of God in salvation, for we do not have salvation without Father, Son, and Spirit. Salvation is of the Lord—singular—and yet it is accomplished by inseparable work of the three persons.

Trinitarian Unity in Salvation

Though there are myriad places to look, Ephesians 1:3–14 provides perhaps the most succinct outline of the Trinity's unified work in salvation. There, Paul lays out a fully Trinity-shaped salvation: the Father bestows salvation and all its blessings, we obtain those blessings through Jesus's work, and the Spirit is the down payment and sealer of those blessings. Moreover, this Trinitarian introduction serves as the hermeneutical key for the rest of Paul's argument in this letter.

First, Paul says that the Father has "blessed us" in Christ, "chose us in him," and "predestined us for adoption" as sons and daughters through him (Eph. 1:3–6). Even as the Father initiates the salvific gifts, he does not act solo. Paul reiterates this later in Ephesians 2:4–7:

> God [the Father], being rich in mercy, because of the great love with which he loved us, even when we were dead in our trespasses, made us alive together with Christ—by grace you have been saved—and raised us up with him and seated us with him in the heavenly places in Christ Jesus, so that in the coming ages he might show the immeasurable riches of his grace in kindness toward us in Christ Jesus.

Notice here that the Father's initiating mercy and love are conjoined to his sending of the Son. According to Paul here, we would not know about the Father's love and mercy were it not for the incarnation and work of the Son. Similarly, Jesus himself says that this love and mercy are why he was sent (John 3:16). When the Jews were flabbergasted at his tendency to make himself equal to God, Jesus did not back down but rather doubled down:

> So Jesus said to them, "Truly, truly, I say to you, the Son can do nothing of his own accord, but only what he sees the Father doing. For whatever the Father does, that the Son does likewise.

For the Father loves the Son and shows him all that he himself is doing. And greater works than these will he show him, so that you may marvel. For as the Father raises the dead and gives them life, so also the Son gives life to whom he will. For the Father judges no one, but has given all judgment to the Son, that all may honor the Son, just as they honor the Father. Whoever does not honor the Son does not honor the Father who sent him. (John 5:19–23)

This is a striking claim from Jesus. He is not merely a subordinate messenger for God; rather, he has the same divine power and authority to know the Father's work fully and even do exactly what the Father does. Because the Father and the Son are equally God in every respect, Jesus is able to say plainly, "Whoever has seen me has seen the Father" (John 14:9). In the Father's sending of the Son, we see the unity of the Father and the Son even as we see their distinction as persons. The eternal life that the Father desires to bestow is found through his sent Son.

Second, Paul transitions to Jesus's work on the cross even as he continues to describe the unified work of the Trinity. Through Christ's shed blood, we finally see the "mystery" of salvation and new creation that had been playing out in human history, which culminated in the cross, where the salvific blessings of grace and mercy were put on full display (Eph. 1:8–10). On the cross, God the Son incarnate was crucified so that we might receive the blessings that the Father wishes to lavish on us. Of course, as Hebrews 12 tells us, the Son went to the cross with joy because he, too, was happy to lavish us with these gifts. As we saw above in Ephesians 2 and John 5, we are made alive by the Father through the Son, yet the Son has the same power to give life.

Paul goes on: "In him we have obtained an inheritance, having been predestined according to the purpose of him who works all things according to the counsel of his will, so that we who were the first to hope in Christ might be to the praise of his glory" (Eph. 1:11–12). As the eternal Son who images the Father and as the firstborn over all creation (Col. 1:15), our adoption as sons and daughters means we receive the inheritance typically due to our older brother. These riches that are so freely lavished on us are not merely the Father's, because any father's riches inherently belong to his family through inheritance. The Father's riches are the Son's riches, and we are adopted into their family as heirs to the same riches, namely, eternal life and communion with the triune God.

Third, Paul does not forget the Spirit, though we may have the tendency to do so. After such a beautiful, sweeping depiction of salvation through the Father and the Son, we are reminded that these blessings would be fleeting without the Spirit: "In him you also, when you heard the word of truth, the gospel of your salvation, and believed in him, were sealed with the promised Holy Spirit, who is the guarantee of our inheritance until we acquire possession of it, to the praise of his glory" (Eph. 1:13–14). The Father's riches, available through the Son, are applied to us by the Spirit as a "down payment" and "sealed" for us. When we make a down payment on a vehicle, for example, we understand that the vehicle belongs to us, but we operate in an already/not yet scenario because we haven't fully received ownership until we have paid out the loan. With the Spirit, however, even in the already/ not yet of a sinful world and as we groan for new creation, we are *already* in Christ, and the Spirit *already* seals us and works on our behalf (Rom. 8:18–27).

Though we are sealed by the Spirit, the Father and the Son do not fade into the background. Jesus told his disciples that the Spirit would be sent by the Father in Jesus's name, in part, to ensure that when Jesus ascends to heaven, they will remember his words (John 14:26). Paul tells us in 1 Corinthians 2 that the Spirit enables us to know the mind of God, and through the Spirit we have the mind of Christ. Later, in his teaching on the importance of our earthly bodies, he asserts:

> But he who is joined to the Lord becomes one spirit with him. Flee from sexual immorality. Every other sin a person commits is outside the body, but the sexually immoral person sins against his own body. Or do you not know that your body is a temple of the Holy Spirit within you, whom you have from God? You are not your own, for you were bought with a price. So glorify God in your body. (1 Cor. 6:17–20)

For Paul, our entire being is wrapped up in the fact that God sent the Spirit to indwell us through the Son's sacrifice, so that we may glorify God. He also says elsewhere, "It is no longer I who live, but Christ who lives in me" (Gal. 2:20). Ephesians 2:18–22 pulls together Paul's thoughts nicely:

> For through [Christ] we both have access in one Spirit to the Father. So then you are no longer strangers and aliens, but you are fellow citizens with the saints and members of the household of God, built on the foundation of the apostles and prophets, Christ Jesus himself being the cornerstone, in whom the whole structure, being joined together, grows into a holy temple in the

Lord. In him you also are being built together into a dwelling place for God by the Spirit.

In sum, where the Spirit is, there also are the Father and the Son. While Father, Son, and Spirit are not each other, they are all equally God, and therefore the Lord's salvation is the Trinity's salvation. This Trinitarian foundation gives us all the benefits of salvation, from justification to glorification. Without the singular will, action, and purpose of our triune God, salvation itself falls apart. Now, let us circle back and discuss in more detail the distinction among the persons in the work of salvation.

Trinitarian Distinction in Salvation

It is clear at this point that we cannot talk about unity without distinction, nor distinction without unity. When we talk about *one* God who saves, we are pressured biblically to talk about the *three* persons. As we have noted many times throughout this book, we cannot elevate the oneness of God over the threeness of God or vice versa. In one of his most famous works, *Of Communion with God the Father, Son, and Holy Ghost*, John Owen beautifully explains the inseparable operations of the persons in our communion with the triune God:

[The Holy Spirit] reveals to the souls of sinners the good things of the covenant of grace, which the Father hath provided, and the Son purchased. He shows to us mercy, grace, forgiveness, righteousness, acceptance with God; letteth us know that these are the things of Christ, which he hath procured for us; shows them to us for our comfort and establishment.[1]

What is communion with God? Simply put, communion with God is the way in which Christians participate in the life and grace of the triune God. So when we discuss the unity of salvation, we are saying with the Bible that God saves and that this affirmation means that Father, Son, and Spirit save us with a singular will, power, and action.

That said, we want to be careful to avoid certain heresies that can creep in. For example, the church fathers addressed this issue as they fought against modalists who taught patripassianism, which is the teaching that the Father himself became incarnate and suffered on the cross. Indeed, this argument was already being addressed by Justin Martyr in the middle of the second century.[2] Salvation is of the Lord, yes, but this Lord is three in one, and thus we must keep a careful balance of unity and distinction while also remembering that there will always be a tension or mystery when describing God.

Staying with our Ephesians 1 outline, we notice that each person of the Trinity has a particular operation or mission within the unified salvific work of God. First, it is the Father whose riches are ready to be lavished upon us. As we mentioned above, as the Father, it is fitting that the inheritance comes from a father, not from a son. The Son is the recipient of this inheritance and is the one who is sent by the Father to bring this inheritance to us.

1 John Owen, *Of Communion with God the Father, Son, and Holy Ghost*, vol. 2, *The Works of John Owen*, ed. William H. Goold (Edinburgh: T&T Clark, n.d.), 239–40.
2 Justin Martyr, *First Apology* 63.

Though equally God in every way that the Father is, it is fitting for the sent Son to be the one bringing us into this family inheritance.

Second, we see that the Son is one who took on flesh, became the obedient second Adam, shed his blood for us, rose bodily from the grave to defeat death, and ascended to the right hand of the Father (Mark 16:19; John 1:14; 1 Cor. 15:20–24; Phil. 2:5–11). And while the Son uniquely puts on flesh among the persons of the Godhead, it is important to maintain that this does not insert disunity or separability into the action of salvation. Quite the contrary, in fact. We see this in considering hypothetical alternatives to the Son's incarnation, for one thing. If the Father had been the one who put on flesh, for example, it would be quite strange to also say that he is sitting at the Father's right hand. Understanding this distinction, then, helps us see the importance of the distinction of persons: to say that the Father died on the cross is to say that the Bible contradicts itself when it says that the Son was sent by the Father or sits at the Father's right hand. When Jesus says elsewhere that he only does and says what the Father does and says (John 5:19; 12:49), he is not saying that it is literally one voice and only one voice, but rather that the Father and the Son are two persons who speak as one, without contradicting each other or being divided. We cannot, then, have salvation without the Father sending the Son, and we cannot know the Father fully without the Son revealing him to us. It is through the Son's incarnation that we receive the salvific blessings of the Father.

Third, and by extension, we cannot have salvation without the work of the Spirit. It is by the Spirit that the Son becomes incarnate through the miraculous conception of the Virgin Mary. It is by the Spirit that the incarnate Son, according to his humanity, is anointed and empowered as Israel's Messiah. The Father and the Son send the Spirit to Christ's church as their advocate, the one who guides them into all truth (John 16:12–15; cf. 14:25–27), distributes gifts to the them (Eph. 4:11–12), and convicts the world of sin, righteousness, and judgment (John 16:8–11) as God's people proclaim the gospel to all nations (Acts 1:8). It is the Spirit, Paul says, who regenerates our hearts through faith and who seals our salvation. Biblically speaking, if the Father sent the Son and the Son did not send the Spirit, then our salvation would not be sealed and the work of salvation would not be completed. Gregory of Nyssa argued that the Spirit is truly God in the exact same way as the Father and the Son because salvation does not happen without the Spirit completing the salvific work of Father and Son.[3] John Calvin says similarly that the "Spirit is the bond by which Christ effectually unites us to himself," and we know that we have no salvation apart from our union with Christ.[4] Put another way, if salvation belongs to the Lord and the Spirit completes the work of salvation, then he must also be the Lord.

"The Father Turned His Face Away"?

We will return now briefly to our discussion in the introduction regarding the crucifixion. The crucifixion is a good case study in showing how a careful Trinitarian framework can help work through thorny issues related to the Trinity and salvation. Not only does it bring to the surface the difficult question of what the Father

---

3   *To Ablabius* 3.1.50.

4   John Calvin, *Institutes of the Christian Religion*, ed. John T. McNeill, trans. Ford Lewis Battles (Philadelphia: Westminster, 1960), 3.1.1.

was "doing" (or not doing) while Jesus hung on the cross, but it also raises the question of the Spirit's seeming absence during the event.

When Jesus quotes Psalm 22 on the cross, "My God, my God, why have you forsaken me?" (Matt. 27:46; Mark 15:34), what does this mean? Thomas McCall helpfully frames the issue surrounding this "cry of dereliction":

> Such a question surely comes from someone who has been unfaithful—and who now blames God for their abandonment. . . . But this question, of course, does not come from someone who has been unfaithful. It does not come from a pious person who simply isn't theologically astute enough to know better. It comes from the lips of none other than Jesus Christ. It comes from the one who *has* been utterly faithful. It comes from the one of whom the Father said, "This is my beloved Son, whom I love; with him I am well pleased" (Mt 3:17). It comes from the one who is the eternal Logos (Jn 1:1), the second person of the Trinity. So these words ring out like a thunderbolt.[5]

Did the Father turn his face away? Put another way, was there some sort of break or rupture between the persons of the Trinity on that fateful day on Golgotha? These answers require carefully handling the biblical text and retrieving sound theological method from the early church. Unfortunately, though a beautiful hymn, lyrics from "How Deep the Father's Love for Us" have perhaps shaped our view of this verse as much as or more than the biblical text and Christian history.

---

5   Thomas H. McCall, *Forsaken: The Trinity and the Cross, and Why It Matters* (Downers Grove, IL: InterVarsity Press, 2012), 13–14.

In popular Christianity, lyrics such as those found in this contemporary hymn are often taken to confirm what many already suspect about the cross, that it is a moment of separation between the Father and the Son. The cry of dereliction in such songs is Jesus's cry of abandonment, meant to communicate an existential angst, a torment of soul rooted in some kind of spiritual distance between the incarnate Son and his heavenly Father due to the latter's wrath being poured out. To say it a bit differently, many view the cross as a moment in which the Father pours out his personal wrath on the Son, and this is felt by the Son at a spiritual level and communicated via the cry of dereliction. Let's briefly work through the issues with the ultimate goal of understanding the unity and distinction in the Godhead. Three considerations help us.

First, there is a Trinitarian consideration: anything we say about the cry of dereliction needs to retain the oneness of the Godhead, both with respect to rejecting any ontological or relational division between Father and Son and with respect to affirming inseparable operations. The cross does not produce division between Father and Son, and it is not only the Father who acts in the crucifixion. It is appropriate to talk about the Father pouring out his wrath, but according to the doctrine of appropriations, ascribing an action to one person of the Trinity does not deny that the other persons are acting inseparably. It is not only the Father that pours out wrath; the Son and the Spirit, as the other two persons of the one God, also pour out the one wrath of the one God. It is, after all, *God's wrath* against sin spoken of all throughout Scripture.

On the other hand, we also remember that the Father sent the Son; he did not send himself. The Spirit was active in the incarnation at conception but did not himself put on flesh. So we need to dispel any notions of other Trinitarian persons dying on the cross. This helps us avoid the ancient heresy of patripassianism—the teaching that the Father himself became incarnate and suffered on the cross. Moreover, since we know that God is immutable and incapable of change (Mal. 3:6; Heb. 13:8), it would certainly jeopardize fundamental affirmations about the doctrine of God to assert that the cross initiated a complete three-day (or even a one-millisecond) loss of Trinitarian relations.

Second, there is a Christological consideration: anything we say about the cry of dereliction needs to retain the oneness of the person of Jesus Christ. He is one person with two natures, divine and human, and he goes to the cross as one person. He is not half God and half man, but rather *fully* God and *fully* man. In other words, the Son cannot die because the divine nature does not die, but nonetheless by virtue of the hypostatic union we can also say that God dies on the cross in virtue of Jesus's humanity. God the Son in his divine nature continued to exist and to sustain the universe. Again, one person of the Trinity could not cease to exist for any time without indicating mutability (changeability) in God's nature, and we know God does not change.

Jesus did, however, die *according to his humanity*, and, as with any human death, his body was separated from his soul/spirit, but his soul/spirit did not cease to exist. In his resurrection, the body and soul/spirit were rejoined, as will ours one day. If we die before he returns, our bodies will be in the ground as we await the resurrection, but we will not cease to exist because our soul/spirit will be in or not in the presence of the Lord (1 Cor. 15; 2 Cor. 5:8). Again, Jesus's body was buried in his descent to the dead, but he didn't cease to exist.[6] Therefore, the human body of God the Son incarnate died, but the hypostatic union of two natures was never separated, broken, or compromised. We affirm that Jesus Christ is the God-man, never ceased to be the God-man in his birth, never ceased to be the God-man in his death and resurrection, now stands ascended in heaven as our mediator as the God-man, and will return one day as the God-man to join our souls/spirits to our resurrected bodies; therefore, we must affirm that God the Son incarnate died that day on Golgotha *in the person of Jesus Christ according to his humanity*, but he in no way, shape, or form ceased to exist or experienced ontological separation from the Father (or Spirit) *according to his divinity*. We know that only the Son receives judgment or is capable of death, because he is the only divine person with a human nature and thus the only divine person capable of suffering and dying, and yet the salvation he secures is the salvation of the one God.

Third, there is a canonical consideration: anything we say about the cry of dereliction needs to retain the canonical unity of Scripture and the covenantal and therefore relational unity between God and his Messiah. Psalm 22 is a lament psalm that *ends with a confession of covenantal hope.* Jesus in quoting Psalm 22 is doing so with the whole psalmic scene in mind; therefore, we shouldn't assume that he is quoting one line of the psalm out of context. Jesus's lament comes in a covenantal context, a context in which he is the messianic Son chosen by Yahweh to deliver his people Israel by suffering on their behalf. God pours out his

---

6 For a full treatment of Jesus's descent to the dead, see Matthew Y. Emerson, *"He Descended to the Dead": An Evangelical Theology of Holy Saturday* (Downers Grove, IL: IVP Academic, 2019).

wrath on Jesus, yes, but as his anointed Son who suffers in his people's place. Further, if we consider the other crucifixion scenes where different portions of Psalm 22 are either quoted or alluded to (e.g., Matt. 27; Mark 15; Luke 23; John 19), we see that they record various ways Jesus fulfills this psalm, pointing us back to the point that Jesus likely had the whole psalm in mind. Finally and perhaps most strikingly, Psalm 22:24 says, "For he has not despised or abhorred the affliction of the afflicted, and he has not hidden his face from him, but has heard, when he cried to him." The afflicted man *is not abandoned* in this text. We see this, in fact, in Jesus's final words on the cross in the other Gospels, where Jesus commends his spirit to the Father (Luke 23:46); promises the thief that he will be with him in "paradise," the place of rest for righteous human souls awaiting the resurrection of the dead (Luke 23:43); and declares the work of salvation finished (John 19:30). So either Jesus is wrong about the Father's abandonment in that moment—to the point of contradicting himself in the aforementioned verses—or something else is going on.

With these guardrails in place, we can offer a rather straight-forward response to our original question: What does Jesus mean when he says this? Most likely, he is identifying with the afflicted King David in Psalm 22. The king has been rejected, persecuted, and scorned; in his suffering, he feels a sense of abandonment, even by God himself. But we know by the end of the psalm that David knows that he is not abandoned. Indeed, he often cries out to God for deliverance, asking God to show himself. In a similar way, Jesus is the Messiah who fulfills the Davidic covenant and therefore identifies with him in this psalm. This answer gives us a much better option than assuming a break in the unbreakable

God, a divide in the undividable God, or a Jesus who is almost literally split in half in his death. Divine simplicity, eternal relations of origin, et al., and a canonical reading of Scripture help us make these distinctions in a more biblically and theologically robust manner. Now, we will take a broader look at the unity and distinction of the Trinity in salvation.

Finally, what was the Spirit "doing" during the crucifixion? A careful reader will note that in Matthew's Gospel, for instance, the Spirit seems to be silent or absent for large chunks of the narrative. Does this mean that he was off taking a heavenly nap? Did he get tagged in for the occasional battle with demons but mostly wait his turn to be sent at Pentecost?

As we've argued throughout this entire book, we should not assume that any person of the Trinity is ever inactive or unneeded. The one God is always at work sustaining the universe, sovereignly reigning over creation, and providentially bringing all things to pass according to his will. Noticeably in Matthew's Gospel, the Spirit is involved in Jesus's conception and birth, his baptism, and his temptation in the wilderness. The entire foundational framing of Matthew's account in the opening chapters shows that the Spirit works inseparably from the Father and the Son in the incarnation. Jesus also says later that he casts out demons by the Spirit (Matt. 12:28). Across the four Gospels, it is easy to point out instances where Jesus casts out demons or performs miracles and the Spirit is not mentioned, but the assumption *should not* be that the Spirit is not present and active in Jesus's ministry, because other portions clearly show that he is. It is best, then, to assume that the Spirit is always at work in the ministry of Jesus and that this foreshadows the sending of the Spirit to the disciples so they can continue the miracle-working ministry by the Spirit in Jesus's name (Luke 10:17; John 14:15–26; Acts 8:6–39). At the crucifixion, then, we can say that the Spirit is still with Jesus, comforting and sustaining him in ways consistent with the Spirit's work in his ministry and the ministry of those who are united to him (Rom. 8).

Beholding the Triune God in Salvation

Salvation, like every other act of God, is the singular act of the one God. This one God exists in three persons, Father, Son, and Spirit, and so the one act of salvation of the one God is also the one act of the triune God. To maintain the unity of this act, we can say, with Scripture, that the Lord saves. To maintain the triunity of this act, we can say, with Scripture, that it is the Father who sends the Son to save us; the Son, who is sent by the Father and becomes incarnate, lives a perfect and vicarious life, dies a penal, substitutionary, atoning, sacrificial death, and rises from the dead on our behalf; and the Spirit is the agent of the Father's sending of the Son as well as the one who anoints and empowers the Son according to his humanity. Salvation belongs to the Lord—the Lord who is Father, Son, and Spirit.

Paul stirringly reminds us of the impact of beholding our triune God in salvation:

Who shall separate us from the love of Christ? Shall tribulation, or distress, or persecution, or famine, or nakedness, or danger, or sword? As it is written,

"For your sake we are being killed all the day long;
we are regarded as sheep to be slaughtered."

No, in all these things we are more than conquerors through him who loved us. For I am sure that neither death nor life, nor angels nor rulers, nor things present nor things to come, nor powers, nor height nor depth, nor anything else in all creation, will be able to separate us from the love of God in Christ Jesus our Lord. (Rom. 8:35–39)

Because of the work of the triune God, our salvation is secured. Nothing in all of creation is stronger than its Creator. And when we are held in the Father's love through the work of the Son and the Spirit, we are bound to the very eternal love of God. What if we dwelled on this truth over and over? What if we fought to believe it? Our triune God has given us everything we need to do just that.

5

Mission

AT THE BEGINNING OF THIS BOOK, we talked about the divine missions—revelations and extensions of the divine processions, the manifestation of divine persons in creation. This term refers to its use in systematic theology, where the doctrine of divine missions is a way of describing God's external works. These missions encompass everything God does external to his own existence, so everything related to creation and redemption.

But in the church's life, *mission* is more often and more specifically a reference to the proclamation of the gospel to the world. It is in this more ecclesial sense, rather than the theological (theology proper) sense, that we use the word in this chapter. How does the Trinity work in the church's proclamation of the gospel?

Trinitarian Unity in Mission

The Trinitarian Source of Mission

God's work in missions is one because he is the source of and empowerment for the church's mission. As we will discuss below, the Bible describes evangelism and missions often in ways that appropriate this work to the Holy Spirit. But we should not mistake appropriation for partition; the Holy Spirit, as the third person of the one God, acts as one with the Father and the Son. We can see this in particular in the language about Pentecost, the historical moment to which we attribute the beginning of the church's mission.

At Pentecost, the Holy Spirit falls upon disciples of Jesus, empowering them for the mission given to them by Jesus in Acts 1:8. So mission is a work of the Holy Spirit, and we affirm this via the doctrine of appropriations below. We should be quick to remember, though, that it is the risen Lord Jesus who promised and who sends the Holy Spirit at Pentecost. Take, for instance, Jesus's promise of the Holy Spirit in John 16:4–15:

> I did not say these things to you from the beginning, because I was with you. But now I am going to him who sent me, and none of you asks me, "Where are you going?" But because I have said these things to you, sorrow has filled your heart. Nevertheless, I tell you the truth: it is to your advantage that I go away, for if I do not go away, the Helper will not come to you. But if I go, I will send him to you. And when he comes, he will convict the world concerning sin and righteousness and judgment: concerning sin, because they do not believe in me; concerning righteousness, because I go to the Father, and you will see me no longer; concerning judgment, because the ruler of this world is judged. I still have many things to say to you, but you cannot bear them now. When the Spirit of truth comes, he will guide you into all the truth, for he will not speak on

his own authority, but whatever he hears he will speak, and he will declare to you the things that are to come. He will glorify me, for he will take what is mine and declare it to you. All that the Father has is mine; therefore I said that he will take what is mine and declare it to you.

This passage has much to unpack. For our purposes, notice first that the Holy Spirit is sent by the Son in order to (1) convict the world and (2) empower the church's proclamation. These are two sides of the same evangelistic coin. God has appointed his church to proclaim the good news of Jesus Christ, and so he sends the Holy Spirit to empower the church to preach the truth (16:12–13). But this preaching is not effective without conviction of sin, righteousness, and judgment, which only God can bring, and so he does through his Holy Spirit (16:8–11). For some, conviction means that they repent of their sins and turn to Christ in faith. For others, though, it means that they harden their hearts against the Lord and his anointed. Either way, conviction is from the Holy Spirit of God, and human preaching is impotent without his empowering and effective work.

Notice also, though, that this empowerment and effectiveness ultimately have their source not in the Spirit alone but in the one God who exists as Father, Son, and Holy Spirit. The Spirit is sent by Jesus (16:7) and his mission is to glorify, or testify to, Jesus (16:14; cf. also 15:26). And Jesus sends his Spirit because he ascends to his Father (16:5, 9), from whom he possesses all things that the Father also has (16:15). The descent of the Spirit happens because of the ascent of the incarnate, risen Son to the Father. The work of the Holy Spirit in the church's mission is ultimately the Trinity's work, from the Father through the Son by the Spirit.

We should also hasten to note that the Holy Spirit in the Bible is the Spirit "of God," "of the Father," and "of Jesus/the Son." Regarding the former, he is named "the Spirit of the Lord" in multiple Old Testament texts, including Isaiah 11:2 and 61:1. With respect to "the Spirit of Jesus/the Christ/the Son," the Spirit is named as such in texts such as 1 Peter 1:11 and Galatians 4:6. The Father also anoints Jesus with the Holy Spirit (Acts 10:38), and the Spirit is called "the Spirit of your Father" by Jesus in Matthew 10:20. The most obvious text to demonstrate the Spirit's unity with the Father and the Son, and their possession of him, John 15:26–27, will be discussed in the final section of this chapter. The point here is that the Holy Spirit, as the Spirit of the Father and of the Son, can never be isolated from the Father and the Son. This means that his actions, and namely here his empowerment of the church's mission, cannot be separated from the one work of empowerment given by the one God who is Father, Son, and Holy Spirit.

The Trinitarian End of Mission

The source of mission, the Holy Trinity, is also the end, or goal, of mission. We are saved by grace through faith *to* communion with the one triune God. Salvation is not just a "get out of hell free" card, or eternal fire insurance (although Christ's work certainly saves those united to him by faith from eternal judgment!). Instead, the aim of salvation is positive—to unite to God in Christ by his Spirit. This goal of mission is exemplified biblically in the Great Commission (Matt. 28:19–20). There Jesus commands the disciples:

> Go therefore and make disciples of all nations, baptizing them
> in the name of the Father and of the Son and of the Holy Spirit,
> teaching them to observe all that I have commanded you. And
> behold, I am with you always, to the end of the age.

Notice that Jesus commands baptism in the *one, singular* name of the three persons of God: Father, Son, and Holy Spirit. Baptism is the sign of the new-covenant reality of union with God, and thus baptism into the one name of the three persons is a sign of union with all three persons of the one God. This signifies the end, or goal, of the church's mission, to see those who were once dead in their trespasses and sins (Eph. 2:1) united to the triune God by faith.

Of course, theologically, this has to be true. For God to be one means that to be united to any one of the persons of God is to be united to all three. So while we can and should appropriate mission to the Spirit, in the sense that he empowers and makes effective the church's witness (see below), it is not only the Spirit to whom we are united by that empowered and effective witness. It is to the Father and the Son and the Spirit that we are united by faith in the Son's work on our behalf. Likewise, to say that the end of mission is "union with Christ" is really to say that we are united to Christ and so also united to the Spirit and the Father. To be in the presence of the Father is also to be in the presence of the Son and the Spirit. And so on. The goal of missions and evangelism is to see lost, sinful persons saved from the wrath of the triune God through the work of the triune God in the incarnation, life, death, resurrection, ascension, and imminent return of his Son and by the power of his Holy Spirit.

The goal of evangelism and missions is everlasting worship of the triune God.

Trinitarian Distinction in Mission

While we must maintain the unity of divine action in mission, another way to answer this question is to appropriate mission to the Holy Spirit. This is appropriate because of the biblical language about the gospel's proclamation and effectiveness. In the book of Acts, as the disciples receive their global commission from the risen Lord Jesus (Acts 1:8), they are told, "You will receive power when the Holy Spirit has come upon you, and you will be my witnesses in Jerusalem and in all Judea and Samaria, and to the end of the earth." The power of the Holy Spirit is necessary for the church's effective witness to the world. This is a programmatic statement for the entire book of Acts; any time the church's witness bears fruit, we should recall why: the power of the Holy Spirit, whom they have received from the risen and ascended Lord Jesus.

The disciples and the rest of the church receive the gift of the Holy Spirit at Pentecost. This foundational event fuels their evangelistic efforts throughout the rest of the book. Anytime, therefore, that the gospel goes to new territory (Jerusalem in Acts 6:7; Judea and Samaria in Acts 12:24; the ends of the earth in Acts 19:20), and is described as "the word of God," "the Lord increased and multiplied," or "prevailed mightily," we should understand that it is through the power of the Holy Spirit. While this is, of course, grounded in the Pentecost event at the beginning of Acts, it is also a fulfillment (as Peter points out in Acts 2) of God's promises to Israel in the Old Testament regarding the gift of the Spirit. Joel 2:28–29, quoted in Acts 2:17–21, says:

And it shall come to pass afterward,
    that I will pour out my Spirit on all flesh;
your sons and your daughters shall prophesy,
    your old men shall dream dreams,
    and your young men shall see visions.
Even on the male and female servants
    in those days I will pour out my Spirit.

God's purposes for sending his Holy Spirit are varied, but the primary emphasis in the new-covenant promises is on a changed heart, i.e., the forgiveness of sins and ability to obey (Jer. 31:31–34; Ezek. 36:25–28). In this passage from Joel, though, the emphasis lies not just on sanctification but on *witness*. The result of having the Spirit poured out onto God's people is that they will testify to him: "your sons and your daughters shall prophesy." The people of God will, through the presence of the Holy Spirit, profess and proclaim to the world the God of Israel who saved them through his Messiah and who can save Gentiles too through faith and repentance. Again, then, in the book of Acts and the rest of the New Testament, we should understand the effective proclamation of the gospel to be the work of the Holy Spirit of God, given by the incarnate, risen, and ascended Son at Pentecost.

This empowerment for prophetic witness by the Holy Spirit is not novel in Acts. The Holy Spirit has always anointed those whom God has appointed to speak and lead, starting (at least) with Moses and the Hebrew elders in Exodus 18, stretching through the preexilic (Samuel, Elijah, Elisha) and exilic and postexilic prophets (e.g., Isa. 61:1–2; cf. 1 Pet. 1:10; 2 Pet. 1:21). This pattern culminates in Jesus Christ, Israel's Messiah, who quotes

Isaiah 61:1–2 and claims he fulfills its promised anointed one: "The Spirit of the Lord is upon me, because he has anointed me to proclaim good news to the poor" (Luke 4:18). Jesus is the prophet par excellence, the one who proclaims God's word faithfully as God the Word enfleshed and anointed, according to his human nature, by God the Holy Spirit.

When Jesus rises from the dead and ascends into heaven, he gives his Spirit to anoint his people: "But when the Helper comes, whom I will send to you from the Father, the Spirit of truth, who proceeds from the Father, he will bear witness about me. And you also will bear witness, because you have been with me from the beginning" (John 15:26–27). Ultimately, the church bears witness to Christ because believers are anointed with the Spirit who proceeds from the Father, the Spirit who bears witness to the Son as the Spirit of the Son and the Father (cf. 1 John 3:24–4:6, 12–16; 5:6–13). His bearing witness culminates in and always refers back to Christ's resurrection from the dead, the Spirit's decisive testimony to Christ's identity as God's Son in the flesh: "[Jesus Christ our Lord] was declared to be the Son of God in power according to the Spirit of holiness by his resurrection from the dead" (Rom. 1:4; see also 1 Tim. 3:16). Thus, the church's mission is really an extension of and empowered by the Spirit's mission (e.g., 1 Thess. 1:5), the Spirit of the Father and the Son who testifies to the Son so that those who are united to him by faith can know the Father.

Another aspect of the church's witness that is attributable to the Holy Spirit in Scripture is its effectiveness. In other words, not only is mission empowered by the Holy Spirit, but it is also only effective through the work of the Holy Spirit. We will not belabor this point, since we have already covered the Spirit's role in salvation in a different chapter. But regeneration, adoption, and calling are all attributed to him. Finally, we should note that the New Testament explicitly mentions the union of Jews and Gentiles, using the metaphor of building God's temple from believers from all nations (cf. 1 Cor. 6) in attribution to the Holy Spirit:

Therefore remember that at one time you Gentiles in the flesh, called "the uncircumcision" by what is called the circumcision, which is made in the flesh by hands—remember that you were at that time separated from Christ, alienated from the commonwealth of Israel and strangers to the covenants of promise, having no hope and without God in the world. But now in Christ Jesus you who once were far off have been brought near by the blood of Christ. For he himself is our peace, who has made us both one and has broken down in his flesh the dividing wall of hostility by abolishing the law of commandments expressed in ordinances, that he might create in himself one new man in place of the two, so making peace, and might reconcile us both to God in one body through the cross, thereby killing the hostility. And he came and preached peace to you who were far off and peace to those who were near. *For through him we both have access in one Spirit to the Father.* So then you are no longer strangers and aliens, but you are fellow citizens with the saints and members of the household of God, built on the foundation of the apostles and prophets, Christ Jesus himself being the cornerstone, in whom the whole structure, being joined together, grows into a holy temple in the Lord. *In him you also are being built together into a dwelling place for God by the Spirit.* (Eph. 2:11–22)

This union of Jew and Gentile is a sign that the gospel is for every tribe, tongue, and nation, crossing ethnic boundaries and spreading across the globe. It is, in other words, an aspect of the church's mission, her mission that is empowered and made effective by the Holy Spirit.

Trinitarian Mission in the Farewell Discourse

We focused our attention earlier on John 16:4–15, a text from Jesus's Farewell Discourse (John 14–17). Here we want to turn to a previous passage in that same discourse, John 15:26–27. In this passage we see both Trinitarian unity in mission and also appropriation of the work of mission to the Holy Spirit. In these verses Jesus says:

> But when the Helper comes, whom I will send to you from the Father, the Spirit of truth, who proceeds from the Father, he will bear witness about me. And you also will bear witness, because you have been with me from the beginning.

Notice first that mission is the work of the one triune God. The first sentence is a densely packed declaration of who God is in himself and to the world. The Spirit is the Helper whom (*ho parakletos hon*) the Son will send. The Spirit is thus the Son's Spirit, possessed by him in eternity and therefore able to be sent by him in the economy of redemption. But the Son does not possess the Spirit on his own; instead, all that the Father has is his (John 16:15). When he sends the Spirit, therefore, he sends him "from the Father" (*para tou patros*, 15:26). Again, ultimately, this sending in God's economic mission is a reflection of his eternal relations of origin, since the Spirit who is sent from the Father is also eternally the Spirit who proceeds from the Father (*ho para tou patros ekporeuetai*, 15:26). Thus whatever this text says about mission, it is ultimately a Trinitarian act—the Spirit who proceeds from the Father and the Son is the same Spirit who is sent from the Father and the Son to be the Helper to the disciples.

This text also affirms, though, that mission is appropriately appropriated to God the Holy Spirit in particular. It is the Holy Spirit who is sent to be the Paraclete, or Helper, to the disciples, after Jesus ascends into heaven. And thus it is the Holy Spirit, "the Spirit of truth," who will "bear witness" to Jesus (15:26). This testimony of the Spirit empowers the testimony of the disciples, who "also will bear witness" (15:27). The Spirit testifies to the Son, fueling the church's testimony to the Son. And the Spirit's empowerment for prophetic witness is also promised, as we saw earlier, in the continuing discourse of 16:4–15. The Spirit who proceeds from the Father and the Son testifies to the Son through the church, which he empowers in its witness to the Son.

Beholding the Triune God in Mission

Mission is an all-encompassing term that refers to the church's witness to the world. We most often think of it as evangelism and missions. In any case, witness is, in Scripture, empowered by and ultimately only effective because of God the Holy Spirit. Mission in the Bible is appropriated to the Holy Spirit because the church's mission is an extension of the Spirit's economic mission. In the economy of redemption, the Holy Spirit's mission is to testify to the Son, through whom we see the Father. Thus the church's testimony to the Son is empowered by the Spirit, whose mission is to testify to the Son.

Ultimately, this mission is the outward or external extension of the Spirit's eternal relation of origin. That is, the Spirit eternally proceeds from, or is spirated by, the Father and the Son. He is eternally the Spirit of the Father and the Son. This means that in the economy of redemption, he testifies to those from whom he proceeds. Because the Son is the image of the Father, the Spirit testifies to the Son, in whom we see the Father (John 14:9).

Thus, the mission of the church is ultimately empowered by and effective because of the triune God. Not only do we behold the triune God in the missions of the Son and the Spirit, but we enable others to behold the triune God in our proclamation of the gospel to a lost and dying world. May our beholding of the triune God encourage and empower us to show him to others.

6

Communion

THE DISTINCTION BETWEEN the Creator and his creatures is a chasm broader than the human mind could possibly comprehend. At best, we can affirm that God is eternal, perfect, and self-sustaining. We, on the other hand, are finite, imperfect, and desperately needy. And yet, as God's image bearers, we are so loved that this great chasm has been crossed, most notably in the sending of the Son and the Holy Spirit.

In chapter 1 on the doctrine of revelation, we noted the graciousness of God's self-communication and covenant-making with his people. We know God because God wants to be known. Not only does he want to be known, but he has made himself and his will known to us in a variety of ways, culminating in the Spirit-inspired Scriptures he has left to us Spirit-indwelled people. With Scripture as the center of our life with God and his people, let's further explore the communion we have with our triune God and what it means for our personal and communal lives as Christ's body.

Trinitarian Unity in Communion

The word *communion* might bring to mind the Lord's Supper that Jesus instituted before his death and has been practiced by Christians ever since (Luke 22:7–23; 1 Cor. 11:17–34). We will return to the Lord's Supper in due course, but for now we will discuss the idea of communion more generally. Here is a simple working definition for *communion* in Christian theology: the sharing of fellowship among God and his people.

The eternal communion of Father, Son, and Spirit is the grounds for our communion with him and one another. Our triune God, simple and perfect for all of eternity, has always been the one God who is Father, Son, and Holy Spirit. As we have mentioned many times in previous chapters, the Scriptures witnessed to the incarnation of the Son and the sending of the Spirit long before these events were made manifest in time and space. The Father did not "become" a Father at some point in time when he decided to create the Son with some unnamed heavenly mother. No, this would insinuate that the Father changed at some point, which would deny Scripture's claim that God cannot change (Mal. 3:6). Further, this would insinuate that the Son was created, which would deny Scripture's claim that he is the Creator, not a creature (John 1:1–3; Col. 1:16; Heb. 13:8). Rather, the Father and the Son shared a communion of love with the Holy Spirit in all eternity—indeed, "before the foundation of the world" (John 17:24).

If God truly is one (Deut. 6:4), then we cannot treat the persons as a "team" of disconnected beings or three "members" of a "divine dance." This way of speaking hints strongly at three divine beings who are *one* only by virtue of agreement or a unity of will.

This is basic anti-Trinitarian Mormon theology. Instead, it's more fitting to speak the way the Bible speaks: "God is love" (1 John 4:8). This verse is simple and yet packed with rich Trinitarian theology. God *is* love. He's not a collection of entities or beings who simply love one another, however deeply, which leads them to work together as some sort of heavenly taskforce. He doesn't love sometimes and not love other times. He doesn't wrestle between fluctuating emotions. No, it's much deeper than that—unfathomably so. The best we can make sense of this is to say with John that Father, Son, and Spirit *just are* the one God who exists in an inseparable communion of love. God loves us as an outflow of his very nature—the one who loves perfectly and eternally.

This one God who *is* love exists as three persons who fully and truly are the loving God. Do the three persons love one another? Yes. But we say this only insofar as the Scripture gives us language to distinguish the persons from each other. However, if we exaggerate the *oneness*, we deny that there are three persons who exist in a perfect and pure life of inseparable, mutual love. Moreover, if we exaggerate the *threeness*, we deny that there is one perfect, simple triune God who *just is* love, and replace him with something like three Gods who, like humans, choose to love one another only under the right circumstances or due to certain impulses.

Trinitarian Distinction in Communion

God is love, and the three persons exist in an eternal communion of that love. God the Father is love. God the Son is love. God the Holy Spirit is love. God's love is not a cookie jar any of the persons can reach into when they need an emotional pick-me-up, but rather a divine attribute that belongs to each person as the one God.

That said, we should not deny that there is a real distinction between the persons and a mutual love that exists between them. The Father wasn't lying when he said at Jesus's baptism, "This is my beloved Son" (Matt. 3:17). He didn't start loving the Son at some point in history, but, again, they shared this love before the foundation of the world. And this love overflows to us in the missions of the Son and the Spirit. Drawing on Ephesians 1:3–14, Daniel Treier helpfully shows four ways the communion between the Father and the Son—the *filial communion*—relates directly to our communion with the triune God via the divine missions: (1) Christ's multifaceted communion with God leads to our sanctity and faithfulness; (2) our election is *in* Christ; (3) we are adopted as sons and daughters through the Son; and (4) the Christ-centered nature of the passage reveals the full integration of our salvation through our own communion with God, reassured by the work of the Spirit in us.[1] For our purposes here, the point is clear: the single, perfect, pure communion of love between the persons is poured out on us, as we are loved by the Father because of our union with the Son, whom the Father loves. The love of God is poured out on us by the inseparable work of Father, Son, and Holy Spirit.

Returning to 1 John 4, we can see the distinction of the persons even within this one love of God that has been graciously offered to us:

In this the love of God was made manifest among us, that God sent his only Son into the world, so that we might live through him. In this is love, not that we have loved God but that he loved

---

1 Daniel J. Treier, *The Lord Jesus Christ* (Grand Rapids, MI: Zondervan Academic, 2023), 50–54.

us and sent his Son to be the propitiation for our sins. Beloved, if God so loved us, we also ought to love one another. No one has ever seen God; if we love one another, God abides in us and his love is perfected in us. By this we know that we abide in him and he in us, because he has given us of his Spirit. And we have seen and testify that the Father has sent his Son to be the Savior of the world. Whoever confesses that Jesus is the Son of God, God abides in him, and he in God. So we have come to know and to believe the love that God has for us. God is love, and whoever abides in love abides in God, and God abides in him. (1 John 4:9–16)

The Father has a love for his Son that he wants to give to us. The personal distinctions are clear in the sending language: the Father is the sender and the Son is the sent one. This could imply that God's love is like a package that the Son is merely delivering on his behalf. But, again, it's much deeper and richer than that. Jesus says elsewhere, "I and the Father are one" (John 10:30) and "All that the Father has is mine; therefore I said that [the Spirit] will take what is mine and declare it to you" (John 16:15). Only God can pour out God's love. Only God can give to us the grace and mercy that only God can give. This is why we can say without hesitation that Father, Son, and Spirit are truly the one God, because they alone bring us into their loving communion. As John says in the various passages above, we love one another *because* we have received the love of God through our union with the Son and the Spirit.

Communion with God in Word and Sacrament

Our communion with the triune God finds its flowering in our personal and corporate life as members of Christ's body, the church. There are numerous ways that we may behold our triune God through his work in us as we commune with him. Indeed, the Christian life *just is* communion with God. The work of the triune God through the missions of the Son and the Spirit is the foundation for all Christian life and worship, and this same work of the Trinity gives us the ability to worship and commune with him "in spirit and truth" (John 4:24). So when we consider our personal devotion to God and our participation in the life and liturgy of the church, we can start with the two most time-tested ways that the church has communed with God, both personally and corporately.

Scripture Reading (Word)

As we have discussed throughout this book, Scripture stands at the center of God's revelation to us so that we may know him and his will for us and our salvation. Consider once again Paul's words to Timothy: "All Scripture is breathed out by God and profitable for teaching, for reproof, for correction, and for training in righteousness, that the man of God may be complete, equipped for every good work" (2 Tim. 3:16–17). When you read the words of Scripture, you are reading the very words of God, inspired and illumined by the Spirit. The word translated "breathed out by God" is also translated elsewhere as "inspired by God" (CSB). The word is a combination of the words for *God* and *breath*, which could be literally translated as "God-breathed" (*theopneustos*). The relationship between God's Spirit and his "breath" is often associated with the Spirit in Scripture both grammatically and theologically (e.g., Job 33:4; John 20:22). So the "Spirit-ual" link between those who wrote Scripture by the

Spirit (2 Tim. 3:16) and those who prophesied in the Spirit in Scripture (2 Pet. 1:21) is clear. When we read the words of the prophets and the apostles recorded in Scripture, God communes with his children by the Spirit.

For much of church history, the idea of personal communion with God in the Scriptures has been called *lectio divina* ("divine reading"). In short, because Scripture is "living and active" because of the Spirit's active work through it (Heb. 4:12), we read Scripture not as a dusty old textbook, but as a vibrant, living word from God himself. And not only do we read Scripture, but Scripture reads us as the Spirit searches our hearts and exposes us to the truth (Heb. 4:13). In this "divine reading" we learn knowledge of and about God, of course, but we also commune with him. He speaks to us there in its pages. And we contemplate his words and read in a posture of prayer, begging God to help us hear from him and to be transformed by him. Through the Spirit, we have access to the very mind of God and are given the mind of Christ (1 Cor. 2). As Paul says to Timothy, we have everything we need for life and godliness in the Scriptures.

Reading the Bible should be a personal *and* corporate act. It pierces the individuals' hearts, but it also pierces *our* hearts as Christ's body who is called to take the gospel to the ends of the earth. Not long after the Spirit was poured out at Pentecost, the church began to gather together to "[devote] themselves to the apostles' teaching" (Acts 2:42). Judging by Jesus's commitment to Scripture and the apostles' writings in the New Testament, what else could we assume the church learned from the apostles except teachings on Scripture and perhaps teachings that were later written down as Scripture?

Baptism and the Lord's Supper (Sacrament)

In the baptism of Jesus (Matt. 3:13–17) and the baptismal formula of the Great Commission (Matt. 28:19), the doctrine of the Trinity is perhaps most clearly taught. As Hilary of Poitiers said, "What is there pertaining to the mystery of man's salvation that [the baptismal formula] does not contain?"[2] In the baptism of Jesus, we see the one act of baptism carried out by the three persons—the Father speaking from heaven, the incarnate Son in the river, and the Holy Spirit descending on the Son. In the baptismal formula in Matthew 28, we see that disciples are to be baptized in the singular name of the three persons—Father, Son, and Holy Spirit.

Hilary also alludes to an important point that we have made elsewhere in this book: the salvation of the one God can only be explained by speaking of the inseparable work of Father, Son, and Spirit. Baptism is a central act at the center of the Bible's teaching on salvation, so regardless of whether one believes baptism is reserved for professing believers or as a sign for children, baptism is inescapably tied to the biblical teaching on salvation. When a person is baptized, the formula is to be spoken over them: "I baptize you in the name of the Father and of the Son and of the Holy Spirit." This is a personal act in one sense, because an individual is being baptized. But it is also a corporate act, because baptism should be performed in the presence of God's church. In baptism we identify with the death, burial, and resurrection of Christ, as inheritors of the Father's promises in Christ, and walk in those promises and the newness of life given by the Spirit. We

2　Hilary of Poitiers, *On the Trinity* 2.1. English translation from St. Hilary of Poitiers, *The Trinity*, trans. Stephen McKenna (Washington, DC: Catholic University of America Press, 1954), 35.

are baptized into one body—Christ's—by one Spirit, just as the baptismal formula spoken over us carries with it the power of the one triune God (1 Cor. 12:13). We commune with God as we obey his commands to be united with Christ and thus united with the triune God. This is why Paul encourages the Corinthian church with a Trinitarian formula: "The grace of the Lord Jesus Christ and the love of God and the fellowship of the Holy Spirit be with you all" (2 Cor. 13:14).

Just as baptism is a sign of our covenant with the triune God and an act of communion with him, so also the Lord's Supper is a sign and act of communion. However, whereas baptism is a one-time act of initiation into the covenant, the Supper is a continual act of participation in the blessings poured out on us by the triune God. In fact, Paul talks about the Supper as an act of worship, a participation in the ongoing work of God in opposition to pagan sacrifices and meals that come from Satan:

> The cup of blessing that we bless, is it not a participation in the blood of Christ? The bread that we break, is it not a participation in the body of Christ? Because there is one bread, we who are many are one body, for we all partake of the one bread. . . . You cannot drink the cup of the Lord and the cup of demons. You cannot partake of the table of the Lord and the table of demons. (1 Cor. 10:16–17, 21)

It is fashionable for some to describe the elements as "nothing magical or special," which is true enough, but we must be careful not to downplay the work of the triune God in the regular partaking of the Supper. Paul warns here that our taking of the Supper is a participatory act reserved for God alone. Why? Because we commune with the triune God when we worship him through the Supper. Something *active* happens—a participation in Christ's work. The Supper is not merely a *looking back* at an event in the past, though we "do this in remembrance of" Christ (Luke 22:19; 1 Cor. 11:24); it is also an act rooted in *present* and *future* hope. Indeed, not only do we commune with the triune God there at the Table, but we preach an eschatological sermon when we do it: "For as often as you eat this bread and drink the cup, you proclaim the Lord's death until he comes" (1 Cor. 11:26). We take the Supper with confidence that the triune God will deliver on all of his promises.

Beholding the Triune God in Communion

There is but one God who is the God of love, and that eternal, perfect, pure love exists between Father, Son, and Holy Spirit. While we cannot begin to describe the mysterious communion of love between the persons, we know that it exists and has been given to us through the testimony of the Scriptures. Yes, the eternal love shared by the triune God has overflowed to us through the sending of the Son and the Spirit. We have everything we need to commune with God because God himself has made the way.

As we commune with the triune God personally, we confess in the Lord's Prayer that it is our Father in heaven who gives us all we need through the Son and the Spirit. And when we commune with the triune God corporately, we confess the triune God in baptism and through the ongoing confession of the Supper, where we "proclaim the Lord's death until he comes" (1 Cor. 11:26). In the everyday means of word and sacrament, we behold our triune God with all five senses.

7

Sanctification

SANCTIFICATION IS BOTH a declaration that those united to Christ in faith are holy in God's sight and also the process of becoming what we are declared to be through the power of the Holy Spirit. Or, as K. Bockmuehl puts it, "sanctification in the New Testament is seen as a one-time event and as a process, the believers *being* and *becoming* holy and *acting* correspondingly."[1]

The end of sanctification is Christlikeness, which ultimately happens when we see him face-to-face (1 John 3:2) at his return, and that moment is referred to as glorification. We will cover it in a subsequent chapter. In this chapter, we want to explore how God's actions in sanctifying us prior to Christ's return are one, not just attributable to the Spirit or the Son or the Father but properly the work of the one triune God.

---

1   K. Bockmuehl, cited in David Peterson, *Possessed by God: A New Testament Theology of Sanctification and Holiness*, New Studies in Biblical Theology 1 (Downers Grove, IL: InterVarsity Press, 2000), 14.

Trinitarian Unity in Sanctification

As a declaration of holiness, sanctification is a proclamation made by the triune God over sinners who have been justified by faith. As David Peterson says, the term "in the New Testament . . . primarily refers to God's way of taking possession of us in Christ, setting us apart to belong to him and to fulfil his purpose for us."[2] God "taking possession" and "setting . . . apart" are synonymous with a declaration of holiness, and with being justified, since the term *sanctification* in the New Testament assumes an Old Testament background. For Israel, to be sanctified meant they were set apart and declared holy by Yahweh, called and equipped by him to fulfill their mission to be a light to the nations. God's presence in their midst was the purpose for their sanctification and the means by which they continued to be sanctified.[3] This same conceptual background defines the term in the New Testament.

God's work of setting apart his people culminates with the incarnation. In John 10:36, Jesus describes himself as the one "whom the Father consecrated and sent into the world." The word *consecrated* (*hēgiasen*) can also be translated "sanctified," as it is in the NASB. Jesus's sanctification is being set apart and sent by God for a purpose, namely to be Israel's Messiah and the world's Savior. He uses the same verb in his high priestly prayer in John 17 when he asks the Father to "sanctify them in the truth; your word is truth. As you sent me into the world, so I have sent them into the world. And for their sake I consecrate [sanctify; *hagiazo*] myself, that they also may be sanctified in truth" (vv. 17–19). In other

2 Peterson, *Possessed by God*, 27.
3 Peterson, *Possessed by God*, 15–25.

words, the disciples', and thus the church's, sanctification is rooted in Jesus's own sanctification; their being set apart is grounded in Jesus's own unique consecration as Israel's Messiah.

Notice also that Jesus prays that God would sanctify them; it is God's initiative that grounds our sanctification, and, in the context of the Trinitarian missions, it is appropriate to appropriate this initiative, and the direction of Jesus's prayer, to the Father specifically. Another important aspect of Jesus's prayer is that he asks God to sanctify them "in the truth," which, while not an overt reference to the Holy Spirit, is more than likely tied to Jesus's earlier teaching about the Paraclete. In the Farewell Discourse, Jesus refers to the Holy Spirit as the "Spirit of truth" three times (John 14:17; 15:26; 16:13),[4] and, as we saw in chapter 5 on mission, the Spirit's mission is to empower the church for the proclamation of the truth to the world. The high priestly prayer of Jesus in John 17 thus hearkens back to Israel's own sanctification by Yahweh, translating God's possession of his people into a new-covenant mode. Because this sanctification is from the Father through the Son and by the Spirit in this text, as we've seen above, it is also a clearly Trinitarian prayer and action. And because it is from the Father's initiative, through the Son's example and atoning work, and by the Spirit's empowering presence, it is an inseparably Trinitarian act.

In Hebrews 10:10, the author specifically attributes the sanctification of the people of God to the will of God accomplished through Jesus Christ: "By that will [God's; cf. vv. 7, 9] we have been sanctified through the offering of the body of Jesus Christ once for all." Similarly, in 2:10, the author says: "For it was fitting that he,

---

4   Peterson, *Possessed by God*, 30–31.

for whom and by whom all things exist, in bringing many sons to glory, should make the founder of their salvation perfect through suffering. For he who sanctifies and those who are sanctified all have one source." Here Jesus is sanctified, or set apart, by God so that he in turn can be and is the sanctifier of the people of God, itself a work that only God does in the Old Testament (Ex. 31:13; Lev. 20:8; 21:15; 22:9, 16, 32).[5] Additionally, the subsequent passage in Hebrews 10:11–18, and in particular verses 16–18, evokes the new-covenant language of Jeremiah 31:33–34 and the promise of Spirit-filled obedience to God's word.[6] In other words, to be set apart by God through Jesus Christ in the new covenant means that the people of God are filled with the Spirit of God, possessed by God for service in his kingdom, and empowered to obey by his Holy Spirit. Thus, in Hebrews, we once again see the Trinitarian shape of sanctification, from the Father through the Son by the Spirit.

Paul speaks of sanctification this way as well in 1 Corinthians. At the beginning of his letter, he addresses the believers at the church in Corinth as "those sanctified in Christ Jesus" (1:2). He follows this with the declaration that the Corinthian Christians are "called to be saints together with all those who in every place call upon the name of our Lord Jesus Christ, both their Lord and ours" (1:2). The word for "saints" (*hagiois*) here is related to the word for "those who are sanctified" (*hegiasmenois*) in the previous clause. Thus another way to put it would be that those who are sanctified in Christ are called to be—to live—sanctified in Christ. Paul culminates this declaration at the conclusion of that opening chapter, where he also refers to Jesus as he "who became to us wisdom from God,

5 Peterson, *Possessed by God*, 34.
6 Peterson, *Possessed by God*, 34–35.

righteousness and sanctification and redemption" (1:30).[7] Jesus is thus himself sanctification and he who sanctifies the people of God in the new covenant. Christians are called to live sanctified lives because they are sanctified in Christ.

In 1 Corinthians 6:10–11, Paul puts these concepts together with the agency of the Spirit. Although the Corinthians once were sexually immoral, idolaters, adulterers, practicers of homosexuality, thieves, greedy, drunkards, revilers, and swindlers, unable to inherit the kingdom of God (v. 10), they are now those who have been washed, sanctified, and justified "in the name of the Lord Jesus Christ and by the Spirit of our God" (v. 11). The word for "sanctified" is once again related to the root found in 1 Corinthians 1:2 and the other passages in Hebrews and John that we have mentioned. The Corinthians have been set apart by God and declared holy in the name of Jesus and by the power of the Spirit.[8] The name of Jesus is functionally parallel to the "Spirit," who is the Spirit "*of our God.*" Here is another Trinitarian statement about sanctification: the Spirit, who is God because he is God's Spirit, is the one in whom we are sanctified, and being sanctified by him is parallel to being sanctified in Jesus, God the Son incarnate.

Two other passages are worth mentioning,[9] both in Acts:

And now I commend you to God and to the word of his grace, which is able to build you up and to give you the inheritance among all those who are sanctified. (20:32)

---

7 Peterson, *Possessed by God*, 40–42.

8 Peterson, *Possessed by God*, 42–47.

9 I have refrained from exegeting two other texts that use the word *sanctify*: Eph. 5:26–27 and 1 Cor. 7:14. While these are important texts with respect to the wider doctrine of sanctification, they do not directly touch on our topic, namely the inseparable act of the triune God.

But rise and stand upon your feet, for I have appeared to you for this purpose, to appoint you as a servant and witness to the things in which you have seen me and to those in which I will appear to you, delivering you from your people and from the Gentiles—to whom I am sending you to open their eyes, so that they may turn from darkness to light and from the power of Satan to God, that they may receive forgiveness of sins and a place among those who are sanctified by faith in me. (26:16–18)

In the first passage, Paul, speaking to the Ephesian elders, refers to Christians as "those who are sanctified." In the latter, the risen Lord Jesus speaks to Paul on the road to Damascus and commissions him to preach the gospel to the Gentiles so that "they may receive forgiveness of sins and a place among those who are sanctified by faith in me" (26:18). In both texts, the whole church is referred to as "those who are sanctified," presumably by God (the triune God), although no specific agency is mentioned. This hearkens back to the Old Testament context of sanctification, in which Israel was called out by God and declared his holy possession, set apart as a light to the nations.[10] Thus, in the New Testament, it is the triune God who sanctifies his people, calling them out, setting them apart, making them a people of his own possession, and declaring them holy in his sight from the Father through the Son by the Spirit. While sanctification comes with an expectation of change (e.g., 1 Cor. 6:11[11]), the emphasis in the New Testament's use of Trinitarian language to talk about

10 Peterson, *Possessed by God*, 55–58.
11 Peterson, *Possessed by God*, 44–47.

sanctification is on the declarative, possessive aspect of God's action toward us in Christ by his Spirit.

Trinitarian Distinction in Sanctification

Nevertheless, the Bible also appropriates sanctification to the Spirit, and especially with respect to the ongoing, transformative, progressive aspect of God's action toward us in Christ by his Spirit. While the term *sanctification* or related words are not necessarily always used to refer to this progress toward holiness, the theological doctrine of sanctification includes both the declarative and progressive aspects of God's action toward us in setting us apart as his holy possession. And in the New Testament, the divine person most often associated with our progress toward holiness is God the Holy Spirit. He is our Comforter, our advocate, the breath of the Father and the Son who gives us life, just as the breath of God gave life to Adam (Gen. 2:7; John 14:26; 20:22).

One of the most explicit passages in this regard is 1 Peter 1:2, which calls the "elect exiles" (v. 1) to whom Peter is writing those who are "in the sanctification of the Spirit." This sanctification that is *in the Spirit* is "according to the foreknowledge of God the Father" and "for obedience to Jesus Christ and for sprinkling with his blood." The latter two phrases connect the Spirit's sanctification with obedience and sacrifice, which points to the Old Testament background of the term. The former phrase, along with the shape of the sentence in general, gives sanctification a Trinitarian shape. But we should not lose sight of the fact that it is the Spirit specifically to whom this passage appropriates the agency in sanctification.

In addition to this specific mention of sanctification, we also see appropriation to the Spirit in a number of other ways. The

Spirit is the one who builds the church into a holy temple in the Lord, a dwelling place for God (Eph. 2:21–22). Both the word "holy" (*hagios*) and the reference to the temple bring to mind the Old Testament background of sanctification, for only what has been sanctified, or made holy, can enter into God's temple or be used to build it.[12]

The Holy Spirit is also the one who brings about progress in sanctification. He who raised Jesus from the dead also gives life to our mortal bodies (Rom. 8:11), and he, rather than our own fleshly efforts, is the one who can help us to obey God's law (Gal. 3:4). Any obedience on our part is ultimately the "fruit of the Spirit" (Gal. 5:22–23), and he also gives us spiritual gifts by which we are called to build up the body of Christ (1 Cor. 12:1–11; cf. Eph. 4:11–12[13]). He is the Spirit of God who alone with the Father and the Son possesses divine wisdom, and thus is the one who makes us wise for salvation and obedience (1 Cor. 2:1–16). It is "by the Holy Spirit who dwells within us" that we are commanded to "guard the good deposit entrusted" to us (2 Tim. 1:13). In other words, the whole of the Christian life, and in particular our ongoing faithfulness to Christ in word and deed, is appropriated to the Spirit as his work of sanctification.

This is a fitting appropriation (as all biblically rooted appropriation is) because it conforms to the triune God's inner life. The Spirit is the one who draws us to Christ and dwells in our hearts

---

12 See also Peterson, *Possessed by God*, for discussion of the temple and the Holy Spirit in 1 Cor. 6.

13 Interestingly, Eph. 4 appropriates spiritual gifts to Jesus, while 1 Cor. 12 appropriates them to the Spirit. Ultimately, the event of Pentecost and 1 Cor. 12 point us in the direction of appropriating spiritual gifts to the Holy Spirit, but this is yet another example of how the works of God are inseparable.

through faith and thus, in uniting us to himself, unites us to the Father and the Son (see chapter 4 on salvation). But he also continues this union, this dwelling in the presence of God through Jesus Christ, and thereby provides the means of progressive sanctification. If sanctification is both declarative and progressive, both of these aspects occur by the same means—being possessed by and dwelling in the presence of the triune God. And it is the Spirit who brings us into communion and maintains communion with himself and with the Father and the Son.

In many evangelical churches, there is a tendency to describe salvation in a Jesus-centered manner. If someone asks, "How is a person saved?" we may answer along with Paul, "If you confess with your mouth that Jesus is Lord and believe in your heart that God raised him from the dead, you will be saved" (Rom. 10:9). While this biblical statement is obviously true, and while we would certainly agree that salvation has a certain Jesus-centrality in the New Testament, we can also say more—indeed, Paul does say more in this same passage—God the Father raised him from the dead. A few page-flips back to Romans 8 also shows the inseparable work of the Holy Spirit, who is active in the ongoing application of Christ's work as adopted sons and daughters of the Father. The resurrection is also attributed to both Jesus and the Spirit in other places (John 2:21; 5:21–22; 10:18; 1 Pet. 3:18). Did the Father raise Jesus from the dead? Yes. Did Jesus raise himself from the dead? Yes. Did the Spirit raise Jesus from the dead? Yes. This is not a contradiction but rather an affirmation: the persons of the Trinity never act alone. And if we pay attention to the depth, breadth, and richness of the biblical portrait of salvation, we will see time and again that we cannot understand salvation or the ongoing work of sanctification without the work of the Trinity.

This continued communion is the way we are sanctified, being conformed into the image of the Son (Rom. 8:28–29) by continually beholding Christ's image by his Spirit (2 Cor. 3:17–18). And because we are changed into the image of the Son by looking at the Son, it is fitting that the same Spirit who proceeds from the Father and the Son in eternity also is sent by the Son and testifies to the Son in the economy (John 15–16). The Spirit testifies to the Son, and by beholding the Son we are changed by the Spirit into his image.[14] Thus sanctification is both an inseparable work of the triune God and appropriately appropriated to God the Holy Spirit.

The Trinity and Being Made Perfect

A passage where we see both sides of this coin is one we've already mentioned, Hebrews 10:1–18. The entire passage is concerned with sanctification, as the author asks his hearers to consider how someone is made perfect (v. 1): by the law, including its sacrificial system (vv. 1–4, 11), or by Jesus Christ (vv. 5–10, 12–18)? We read that it is not by "sacrifices and offerings and burnt offerings and sin offerings" (v. 8), or by "the blood of bulls and goats" (v. 4), but, we're told in the central verse of the passage (v. 10), by the will of God "through the offering of the body of Jesus Christ once for all" that we are sanctified. Later on, in verse 14, the author repeats this point, saying that Christ "by a single offering . . . has perfected for all time those who are being sanctified."

---

14 On the relation between the Spirit's eternal procession and economic mission, see Fred Sanders, *Fountain of Salvation: Trinity and Soteriology* (Grand Rapids, MI: Eerdmans, 2022), 91–92, 120–28.

To put it simply, it is God who sanctifies us through Christ's atoning work, not our own efforts to obey the law. This puts sanctification in the hands of God rather than the hands of human beings, and it is from the will of God through the incarnate Son. This is in one sense, then, a kind of "binitarian" description of sanctification, from the Father through the Son. But that would only be the case if we stopped at verse 14. Verses 15–18, though, include the Spirit in the work of sanctification, and, in fact, appropriate the entire work to him:

And the Holy Spirit also bears witness to us; for after saying,

> "This is the covenant that I will make with them
>   after those days, declares the Lord:
> I will put my laws on their hearts,
>   and write them on their minds,"

then he adds,

> "I will remember their sins and their lawless deeds no more."

Where there is forgiveness of these, there is no longer any offering for sin.

Notice that in these final verses of this passage, the author appropriates the entire work he has just been describing to the third person of the Trinity. The Holy Spirit "bears witness" and speaks (v. 15), and is thus the one who uses the personal pronoun "I" in verses 16 and 17. It is therefore the Holy Spirit who speaks Jeremiah 31:33–34, and via prosopological exegesis is therefore the one who puts his law on his people's hearts and writes it on their minds (Heb. 10:16; cf. Jer. 31:33) and also the one who remembers "their sins and their lawless deeds no more" (Heb. 10:17; cf. Jer. 31:34).

This double effect of sanctification—the declaration of holiness (forgiveness + sinlessness) via divine possession, and the ability to obey via the indwelling of the Holy Spirit—is, for the author of Hebrews, specifically the work of the Holy Spirit in Hebrews 10:16–17. And because of the work of the Spirit in this regard, "there is no longer any offering for sin" (v. 18); that is, there is no longer any need for the offerings required under the Torah (vv. 1–4, 11). In this entire passage, then, the author of Hebrews demonstrates that sanctification is both a Trinitarian work, inseparably from the Father through the Son by the Spirit, and also a work specifically appropriated to the Holy Spirit.

Beholding the Triune God in Sanctification

In the New Testament, the work of sanctification is God's declaration that the church is his holy possession, set apart by him for mission to the world. This declaration of holiness comes with an expectation of growth in holiness, progress in obedience to the Lord. While the former is often attributed to the Godhead, or more specifically to the will of the Father through the work of the Son, the latter is most often appropriated to the Holy Spirit. This is fitting, because the Spirit's mission is to testify to the Son, and by beholding the Son we are transformed into his image to the glory of the Father. Because the Spirit is the Spirit of the Father and the Son, proceeding from Father and Son eternally, it is fitting to his eternal relation of origin that his mission in the economy is to testify to the one from whom he proceeds.

Sanctification requires us to live a life of repentance in Christ and bears the fruit of the Spirit in our words and deeds (Gal. 5:16–26). And one beautiful result of sanctification is being able to behold the triune God in the life change that we experience. As Paul says elsewhere, "And we all, with unveiled face, beholding the glory of the Lord, are being transformed into the same image from one degree of glory to another. For this comes from the Lord who is the Spirit" (2 Cor. 3:18). When we behold the triune God, we are transformed by the triune God. When we are transformed by the triune God, we behold the triune God who transforms us. This cycle is not vicious, but rather glorious, freeing, and life-giving.

8

Judgment

"JUDGE NOT, THAT YOU BE NOT JUDGED" (Matt. 7:1). This verse is sometimes used in response to someone being confronted with their sin. Of course, for the church, judgment can be necessary as a means to restoration (1 Cor. 5). The problem Jesus addresses in Matthew, however, is the human tendency to believe that we have the power and wisdom to judge all matters, or to know the appropriate judgment God himself would dole out. But the triune God's judgment is more than wrath (though it is not less than that); it is also an act of love, justice, and even mercy. And the simple triune God's judgment is not divided into emotional parts—anger at times, love or forgiveness other times. The cross is the most obvious example: at the cross, God's holy wrath toward sin, love and mercy for sinners, and justice toward evil are all on display in the same act at the same time.

Speaking of the cross, the three ecumenical creeds specifically mention judgment as the last of the incarnate Son's works, each saying, "He will come again to judge the living and the dead." In one sense, then, it is appropriate to appropriate divine judgment to the Son. And we will see in our survey of biblical language below that this fits the pattern of Scripture's own speech about the last judgment. But as with all of God's acts, judgment is ultimately an act of the one God, the God who is triune. Scripture refers to the final judgment as an act not of the Son alone but also of the Father and the Spirit.

Trinitarian Unity in Judgment

There are numerous passages throughout the Bible that deal with final judgment, including ones that refer simply to the one God as judge. These include Psalm 9:7–8, which says:

> But the Lord sits enthroned forever;
>> he has established his throne for justice,
> and he judges the world with righteousness;
>> he judges the peoples with uprightness.

Similarly, Qohelet ends his sermon, in part, with a promise of divine judgment in Ecclesiastes 12:14:

> For God will bring every deed into judgment, with every secret thing, whether good or evil.

Many passages of Scripture concerning divine judgment, and especially the ones we will consider in relation to its Trinitarian shape, are clustered in a few specific books: Daniel, the four Gospels, and Revelation. Of course, we could also discuss and exegete those many other verses in Scripture that deal with final judgment, especially in the Major Prophets and in the New Testament Epistles. Here, though, our purpose is not to give a fully orbed biblical theology of final judgment but to explore passages that help us understand final judgment as an inseparable operation of the Holy Trinity. And in that regard, the major apocalyptic material of the Bible, and namely that included in the books of Daniel, the Synoptic Gospels, and Revelation, helps us tremendously in that regard.

First, in Daniel, the vision of chapter 7 centers on Yahweh's judgment of four monstrous beasts, each of whom represents earthly kings and their kingdoms. These are each judged by the Ancient of Days (Yahweh, or "the Most High" in vv. 22, 25), in verses 9–12. He is described as sitting on his throne and, in appearance,

> his clothing was white as snow,
>   and the hair of his head like pure wool;
> his throne was fiery flames;
>   its wheels were burning fire. (7:9)

As he sits in judgment (as opposed to those who stand before him to be judged, 7:10), he opens "the books" that serve as his basis for that judgment (see also 12:1–2). After his judgment of the four beasts (7:11–12), the Ancient of Days is joined by another figure, "one like a son of man" (7:13). This son of man's authority is equal to the Ancient of Days, since, as Daniel describes:

> And to him was given dominion
>   and glory and a kingdom,
> that all peoples, nations, and languages
>   should serve him;

his dominion is an everlasting dominion,
    which shall not pass away,
and his kingdom one
    that shall not be destroyed. (7:14)[1]

Judgment in Daniel 7 is thus exercised by *both* the Ancient of Days and the son of man, represented in verses 9–10 in the Ancient of Days opening the books of judgment and in verses 13–14 in the son of man possessing dominion over all earthly kingdoms and authorities.

In the Gospels, Jesus regularly uses the title "Son of Man" to identify himself. Sometimes, this is merely a phrase that indicates his common humanity with those he came to save, but sometimes it is a specific reference to the son of man of Daniel 7:13–14.[2] This is particularly true of the Olivet Discourse passages (Matt. 24; Mark 13; and Luke 21), in which Jesus teaches the disciples about the end of the age. This includes teaching concerning final judgment, and it is in that respect that Jesus uses the title "Son of Man" (e.g., Mark 13:24–27). Thus, according to the *analogia fidei* ("analogy of faith"), we should understand the son of man in Daniel 7 to be God the Son. In that case the Ancient of Days should be identified as God the Father.

---

1 This is a controversial passage, and the interpretation I've given—that the son of man is equal to the Ancient of Days—is probably the minority among biblical scholars. Nevertheless, there are good exegetical reasons for holding to such a position. See, e.g., G. K. Beale, *A New Testament Biblical Theology: The Unfolding of the Old Testament in the New* (Grand Rapids, MI: Baker Academic, 2011), 191–92.

2 James Edwards's overview of the use of "Son of Man" in the Gospel of Mark is a good introduction to the issue and to the understanding of the phrase I am taking here. See James R. Edwards, *The Gospel according to Mark* (Grand Rapids, MI: Eerdmans, 2002), 79–81.

But it is not quite so easy as that, since in Revelation 1 Jesus is depicted as *both* the Ancient of Days *and* the Son of Man. John names him "one like a son of man" in Revelation 1:13, echoing Daniel 7:13, but then also describes Jesus thusly:

> The hairs of his head were white, like white wool, like snow. His eyes were like a flame of fire, his feet were like burnished bronze, refined in a furnace, and his voice was like the roar of many waters. (Rev. 1:14–15)

This is a clear allusion to Daniel 7:9–10 and Daniel's description of the Ancient of Days, especially with respect to having hair "like pure wool" (Dan. 7:9) and "eyes . . . like a flame of fire" (cf. Dan. 7:10, "a stream of fire issued and came out from before him"). John thus describes Jesus using language that connects him to both the son of man and the Ancient of Days. Perhaps this is a way to refer to Christ's two natures, human (son of man) and divine (Ancient of Days). If so, John is quoting Daniel 7 not only with respect to its Trinitarian implications, as he certainly throughout the book refers to all three divine persons distinctly and with equality,[3] but also in support of Christ's two natures.

In any case, John's description of Jesus as the Ancient of Days helps us understand Daniel 7:9–14 as referring to a plurality of divine persons. As we said above, in Daniel's time of writing and for his audience, the Ancient of Days, the Most High, would have been understood to be Yahweh. John is thus identifying Jesus with

---

3 See Brandon D. Smith, *The Trinity in the Book of Revelation: Seeing Father, Son, and Holy Spirit in John's Apocalypse*, Studies in Christian Doctrine and Scripture (Downers Grove, IL: IVP Academic, 2022), esp. 96–106.

the God of Israel, and thus indicating a plurality of persons within the Godhead. For our purposes, this means that both Daniel 7 and Revelation teach that judgment is Trinitarian in shape, from the Father through the Son.

This is not the only place in Revelation where we see judgment portrayed in Trinitarian terms. Among other places, in Revelation 4–5 we see a throne-room scene in which God sits in judgment over the earth. "The Lord God Almighty" (Rev. 4:8) is enthroned in heaven, and with him is "the seven spirits of God" (Rev. 4:5), who is the Holy Spirit.[4] He sits in authority over the forces of evil, represented by the sea of glass (Rev. 4:6a), as well as over creation, represented by the four living creatures (Rev. 4:6b–8), and the church, represented by the twenty-four elders (Rev. 4:9–11). He also, in his right hand, holds "a scroll written within and on the back, sealed with seven seals" (Rev. 5:1). As will become apparent in chapter 6, and also via the allusion to the mentions of scrolls in the Old Testament Prophets, this scroll is a scroll of judgment. And the one worthy to open it is "the Lion of the tribe of Judah, the Root of David" (Rev. 5:5), who appears to the congregation as "a Lamb standing, as though it had been slain" (Rev. 5:6). Notably, this Lion-Lamb, who readers should recognize as Jesus Christ, also possesses "seven horns and . . . seven eyes, which are the seven spirts of God sent out into all the earth" (Rev. 5:6). In other words, God in chapter 4 and the Lion-Lamb in chapter 5 each possess the same "seven spirits of God," who is the Holy Spirit. Thus, as the Lion-Lamb takes the scroll from the Lord Almighty, the Spirit is present in this initial act related

4 Smith, *The Trinity in the Book of Revelation*, 151–65.

to divine judgment in the book of Revelation. Judgment is, from the beginning, a Trinitarian act, from the Father ("the Lord God Almighty," Rev. 4:8) through the Son, who takes the scroll (Rev. 5:7) and is worthy to open it (Rev. 5:9; 6:1ff.), by the Spirit, who is possessed by and present with the Father and the Son (Rev. 4:5; 5:6). Both Daniel and Revelation, then, ultimately see divine judgment as an act carried about by the Holy Trinity.

This unity in Trinitarian action is also seen in John's descriptions of judgment in the Fourth Gospel. First, in John 5, Jesus describes his relation to the Father through reference to a number of different divine actions and attributes, including judgment. The point in each of these is that the Son does what the Father does because he is the Son of the Father. To speak in Nicene terms, John 5 teaches that the Father has communicated to the Son—eternally—the divine essence, thereby also granting the Son the authority and ability to perform divine actions alongside the Father. Regarding judgment, Jesus refers to this divine act twice, both in verse 22 and in verses 27–29. The latter has parallels with Daniel 7 and 12:

> And [the Father] has given him authority to execute judgment, because he is the Son of Man. Do not marvel at this, for an hour is coming when all who are in the tombs will hear his voice and come out, those who have done good to the resurrection of life, and those who have done evil to the resurrection of judgment.

In this passage, it is the Father who judges through the Son. But John does not leave the Spirit out of this divine action in his Gospel; in John 16:8–11, Jesus teaches:

When [the Paraclete] comes, he will convict the world concerning sin and righteousness and judgment: concerning sin, because they do not believe in me; concerning righteousness, because I go to the Father, and you will see me no longer; concerning judgment, because the ruler of this world is judged.

This completes the Trinitarian portrait of judgment in John's Gospel, as here Jesus teaches that it is by the Spirit that judgment is meted out onto the world. Judgment is Trinitarian in shape, in Daniel, in Revelation, and in the Fourth Gospel, from the Father through the Son by the Spirit.

Trinitarian Distinction in Judgment

As with other divine actions, there are passages that speak of Trinitarian unity and others that speak of Trinitarian distinction in judgment. In the Old Testament, focus is occasionally on the role of the Holy Spirit in judgment, and in particular in the resurrection of the dead. Although this particular action is often associated with salvation, as it should be, it also is appropriately connected to judgment. As Revelation 20:11–15 depicts, God's eschatological, final judgment raises the dead, both the righteous and the unrighteous, to everlasting life or death, respectively (see also Dan. 12:1–2). And, according to Scripture, the Spirit is the divine agent of this general resurrection of the dead. For instance, in Ezekiel 36 and 37, when Yahweh promises new life to Israel, it is through the agency of the Holy Spirit that God's people will finally be able to obey (Ezek. 36:27) and, ultimately, to live, having been raised from the dead by the Lord through his Spirit (Ezek. 37:14). This agency of the Holy Spirit in resurrection is echoed in the New Testament in, for instance, Romans 8:11, where Paul reminds us that "the Spirit of him who raised Jesus from the dead dwells in you," and because of this indwelling of the Spirit we can be assured that one day, at the final judgment, "he who raised Christ Jesus from the dead will also give life to your mortal bodies through his Spirit who dwells in you."

Perhaps most often in Scripture, though, Trinitarian distinction with respect to judgment focuses on the actions of the incarnate Son. Jesus prophesies in his Olivet Discourse in the Synoptic Gospels that one day soon he will return in judgment. In Matthew 24:29–31 (cf. Mark 13:24–27; Luke 21:25–28), he describes the final judgment this way:

> Immediately after the tribulation of those days the sun will be darkened, and the moon will not give its light, and the stars will fall from heaven, and the powers of the heavens will be shaken. Then will appear in heaven the sign of the Son of Man, and then all the tribes of the earth will mourn, and they will see the Son of Man coming on the clouds of heaven with power and great glory. And he will send out his angels with a loud trumpet call, and they will gather his elect from the four winds, from one end of heaven to the other.

It is the incarnate Son who initiates and executes divine judgment in this passage. The same is true of the depictions of judgment in Revelation 19 and 20. John describes the beginning of the final judgment this way, in Revelation 19:11–21:

Then I saw heaven opened, and behold, a white horse! The one sitting on it is called Faithful and True, and in righteousness he judges and makes war. His eyes are like a flame of fire, and on his head are many diadems, and he has a name written that no one knows but himself. He is clothed in a robe dipped in blood, and the name by which he is called is The Word of God. And the armies of heaven, arrayed in fine linen, white and pure, were following him on white horses. From his mouth comes a sharp sword with which to strike down the nations, and he will rule them with a rod of iron. He will tread the winepress of the fury of the wrath of God the Almighty. On his robe and on his thigh he has a name written, King of kings and Lord of lords. Then I saw an angel standing in the sun, and with a loud voice he called to all the birds that fly directly overhead, "Come, gather for the great supper of God, to eat the flesh of kings, the flesh of captains, the flesh of mighty men, the flesh of horses and their riders, and the flesh of all men, both free and slave, both small and great." And I saw the beast and the kings of the earth with their armies gathered to make war against him who was sitting on the horse and against his army. And the beast was captured, and with it the false prophet who in its presence had done the signs by which he deceived those who had received the mark of the beast and those who worshiped its image. These two were thrown alive into the lake of fire that burns with sulfur. And the rest were slain by the sword that came from the mouth of him who was sitting on the horse, and all the birds were gorged with their flesh.

Once again, it is the incarnate Son who initiates and executes divine judgment, and in this scene it is against all enemies of God, and especially against the beast and the false prophet. A parallel passage occurs in the next chapter, where the incarnate Son sits in divine judgment over all the dead and, ultimately, over the dragon and Death and Hades:

> Then I saw a great white throne and him who was seated on it. From his presence earth and sky fled away, and no place was found for them. And I saw the dead, great and small, standing before the throne, and books were opened. Then another book was opened, which is the book of life. And the dead were judged by what was written in the books, according to what they had done. And the sea gave up the dead who were in it, Death and Hades gave up the dead who were in them, and they were judged, each one of them, according to what they had done. Then Death and Hades were thrown into the lake of fire. This is the second death, the lake of fire. And if anyone's name was not found written in the book of life, he was thrown into the lake of fire. (Rev. 20:11–15; see also Rev. 21:8)

Again, it is the incarnate Son who initiates and executes divine judgment. He is the one who sits on the throne (cf. Rev. 20:4) and who distinguishes between the righteous and the unrighteous and sends them to their eternal reward, the former to everlasting life and the latter to everlasting death. This focus on the incarnate Son's role in judgment is ultimately a reflection of the Trinitarian shape of divine action—from the Father through the Son by the Spirit. Judgment is through the Son, but that does not preclude the Father's and the Spirit's action in it. The focus on the Son is also a way to highlight God's fulfillment of his promises to Israel.

Jesus, the incarnate Son, is fully divine and fully human, and, as the fully human Messiah of Israel, the Son of David, he executes divine judgment over all the kingdoms, kings, and citizens of the earth (Ps. 2:7). Ultimately, it is the triune God who judges, but Scripture appropriately sometimes appropriates this action to the Son in particular, as Israel's Messiah and as the image of the Father and his authority.

Trinitarian Judgment at the Eschaton

A passage that highlights both Trinitarian unity and distinction is 1 Corinthians 15:26. It is also a passage that can be, on its face, read in such a way to provide proof *against* inseparable operations. But the latter would be a grave interpretive mistake. In this passage, Paul is comparing the *humanity* of Adam and Jesus, the former as the first head of humanity and its fall into sin and the latter the head of the new humanity through his death and resurrection:

> For as by a man came death, by a man has come also the resurrection of the dead. For as in Adam all die, so also in Christ shall all be made alive. (15:21–22)

Paul continues in this train of thought by pointing to the final judgment, when Christ's own resurrection will bring about the resurrection of the faithful to everlasting life: "But each in his own order: Christ the firstfruits, then at his coming those who belong to Christ" (15:23). This reference to the general resurrection leads Paul to describe the final judgment in the following verses (15:24–28) in this manner:

Then comes the end, when he delivers the kingdom to God the Father after destroying every rule and every authority and power. For he must reign until he has put all his enemies under his feet. The last enemy to be destroyed is death. For "God has put all things in subjection under his feet." But when it says, "all things are put in subjection," it is plain that he is excepted who put all things in subjection under him. When all things are subjected to him, then the Son himself will also be subjected to him who put all things in subjection under him, that God may be all in all.

Some have taken verses 27–28 to mean that God the Son *as God* is in some way subordinate to God the Father. The problem with this interpretation is at least twofold. First, it ignores the context, mentioned above, in which Paul is comparing the *humanity* of Adam and Jesus. To rip verses 27–28 out of this context and suddenly make them references to the deity of Jesus is a mistake. It is a mistake exacerbated by another aspect of the passage's context, namely the Old Testament quotation in verse 27. Here, Paul quotes and interprets Psalm 8:6, a psalm that clearly and exclusively concerns humanity and, in particular, humanity's role as image bearer of God and, thus, representative of God's authority. When Paul speaks, then, of the Son delivering "the kingdom to God the Father" (1 Cor. 15:24), and when he says that "the Son himself will also be subjected to him who put all things in subjection under him, that God may be all in all" (15:28), it is important that we keep both the immediate and canonical context in mind. Paul is not speaking indiscriminately of the Son, either holistically or partitively according to his divinity, but partitively according to his humanity.[5]

This means that the proper reading of this passage is both one of Trinitarian unity and of Trinitarian distinction. Regarding Trinitarian unity, it is the one God who "put all things . . . under his feet" (15:27; cf. Ps. 8:6). Regarding Trinitarian distinction, there is Trinitarian *taxis*, or order, to this divine action, namely that judgment comes from the Father through the incarnate Son. In particular, the incarnate Son according to his humanity submits to God, appropriately appropriated specifically to God the Father but in reality to the entire Trinity. We could say, then, that final judgment is the incarnate Son according to his humanity submitting the kingdom, the kingdom which he purchased with his own death and resurrection, to himself according to his divinity, along with the Father and the Spirit. Once again, inseparable operations, appropriations, and partitive exegesis help us rightly divide the word of truth.

Beholding the Triune God in Judgment

While judgment is often thought of as an act of an angry Father God up in heaven, the doctrine of inseparable operations allows us to see a fuller picture of Scripture's depiction of the triune God as the judge of the living and the dead. And this judgment brings with it true justice. If God turned a blind eye to sin, there would be no justice for the innocent and the abused. If God was recklessly vengeful and vindictive toward sin, there would be no place for his love for sinners and his mercy toward them. In the

---

5 See on this Basil of Caesarea, *Against Eunomius* 6.13; and Augustine of Hippo, *De Trinitate* 1.15, 20, 28.

triune God's judgment, we behold his holiness, his justice, his goodness. We can rest in the truth that our eternal blessedness with him will include the eradication of Satan, sin, and the ever-reaching consequences Satan and sin have brought on the world (Rev. 21–22).

Glossary

Appropriation. Our ability to assign one act or attribute of God to a particular divine person while recognizing that the act or attribute to which we're referring actually belongs equally to all three at once, because they are the one God. So although the entire Godhead performs every divine act (see Inseparable operations), sometimes the Bible appropriates that act to only one of the divine persons.

Economy (Economic) and *Ad Extra*. God's acts that are external to his existence, most notably with respect to creation and redemption. When the terms *ad extra* or *economy* or *economic* are used, they distinguish God's activity in creation and salvation from who he is apart from those acts (see Ontology [Ontological] and *Ad Intra*).

Eternal generation of the Son. The first procession in God's life is the eternal generation of the Son by the Father. The Father eternally (i.e., never starting and never stopping) communicates the divine essence to the Son. This means that the Son has always been and always will be God because he is eternally the Son of the Father by nature.

Eternal relations of origin. The only distinction between the divine persons that exists apart from their economic missions. The Father, the Son, and the Holy Spirit are distinguished from one another eternally via relations to one another (see also *Taxis*).

Eternal spiration of the Spirit. The second procession in God's life is the eternal spiration of the Spirit by the Father and the Son. The Father and the Son eternally (i.e., never starting and never stopping) communicate the divine essence to the Spirit. This means that the Spirit has always been and always will be God because he is eternally the Spirit of the Father and the Son.

Inseparable operations. Every act of God is an act of the three persons of the one God, even when the Bible sometimes refers to only one of the persons as performing that act (see Appropriation).

Missions. The divine missions are revelations and extensions of the divine processions, the manifestation of divine persons in creation. So, for example, in the incarnation, the Father, who is eternally ingenerate, sends the Son, whom he eternally generates, and he sends him by the Spirit, who eternally proceeds from the Father and the Son.

Ontology (Ontological) and *Ad Intra*. God's acts that are internal to his existence, most notably with respect to his eternal relations of origin. When the terms *ad intra* or *ontological* are used, they distinguish God's nature or inner life, i.e., who he is in himself apart from any other work, from his activity in creation and salvation (see Economy [Economic] and *Ad Extra*).

Person. Distinguishes Father, Son, and Holy Spirit from one another. Each person of the Trinity is not a "part" of a divided God, but rather a "someone" who subsists within the one, simple divine nature or essence. There is one God (one divine nature) and three fully divine persons, Father, Son, and Holy Spirit.

Processions. There are two processions: the Son being generated eternally from the Father, and the Spirit being spirated eternally from the Father and the Son.

Simplicity. Asserts the absolute unity of the Trinity. The Father, the Son, and the Spirit are not "parts" of God as though they each make up one-third of God's nature or essence. All of God's attributes are shared equally and fully by each person of the Trinity, for the triune God is not a created being that was put together by a greater Creator, but rather is eternally the one God in three persons.

Taxis (**Order**). The order of God's inner life and also his external works, and namely that both are from the Father, through the Son, by the Spirit. This order is not an indication of priority or ranking within the Godhead, but instead is an acknowledgment that the three persons of God are distinguished by their relations of origin, which are subsequently reflected in God's economic activity. Every act of God, because of who God is as Father, Son, and Spirit, is *from* the Father *through* the Son and *by* the Spirit. And this *from-through-by* language does not indicate a hierarchy, but rather a unified order.

General Index

Scripture Index